A Friendly Guide to THE PROPHETS

BRIAN BOYLE

garratt PUBLISHING

Published in Australia by
Garratt Publishing
32 Glenvale Crescent
Mulgrave, Vic. 3170

www.garrattpublishing.com.au

Text Copyright © Brian Boyle
Images Copyright © iStock
Design by Lynne Muir

First published 2015

All rights reserved. Except as provided by the Australian Copyright Law, no part of this book may be reproduced in any way without permission in writing from the publisher.

9781925009613

Scripture quotations are drawn from the *New Revised Standard Version of the Bible*, copyright © 1989 by the Division of Christian Education of the National Council of the Churches of Christ in the USA. Used by permission.

Cataloguing in Publication information for this title is available from the National Library of Australia.
www.nla.gov.au

Every effort has been made to trace the original source of copyright material contained in this book. The publisher would be pleased to hear from copyright holders to rectify any errors or omissions.

Contents

GETTING STARTED   3

INTRODUCTION   4

CHAPTER ONE   **ISRAEL'S PROPHETS**   10
   Who were the Prophets?   10
   Features of a prophet   11
   When and why did prophecy emerge in Israel?   13
   What did prophets preach about?   14
   How can you tell if prophecy is true?   16
   Jesus as prophet   16

CHAPTER TWO   **AMOS – A ROARING LION**   18
   The prophet Amos and the socio-economic context of his preaching   19
   A snapshot of the prophet Amos   19
   The structure of the Book of Amos   20
   Prophetic language and imagery of Amos   21
   The message of Amos: religion is no substitute for justice   21
   The vision reports of Amos (7:1-9; 8:1-3)   21

CHAPTER THREE   **HOSEA – THE ENDURING LOVE OF GOD**   26
   The prophet Hosea and the religious context of his preaching in Israel   27
   The structure of the Book of Hosea   27
   What is it the Lord really wants?   29
   The poetic language and imagery of Hosea   30
   Hosea 11:1-11, a classic text of God's parental and nurturing love for Israel   32

CHAPTER FOUR   **JEREMIAH – RELUCTANT PROPHET**   34
   The prophet Jeremiah and the religious and political context of his preaching   35
   Jeremiah's life and ministry as witness of his troubled times   37
   The structure of the Book of Jeremiah   38
   A celebrated Jeremiah text 31:31-34: the new covenant   39

CHAPTER FIVE   **EZEKIEL – DIVINE PRESENCE IN ABSENCE**   42
   Ezekiel: prophet of exile   43
   An outline of the Book of Ezekiel   43
   The Book of Ezekiel as trauma literature   44
   A vision of hope: the bones in the valley (37:1-14)   46

CHAPTER SIX   **ISAIAH AND HIS CHILDREN**   48
   Isaiah and the Messiah   49
   Children in messianic texts   49

CONCLUSION   52

MODERN PROPHETS   54

GLOSSARY   56

Getting Started

The *Introduction* and *Contents* will give the reader an outline of the scope and purpose of this book. I would like to make some general comments and suggestions to the reader as they take up this book on the fascinating phenomenon of prophecy in ancient Israel.

The translation used is the *NRSV* (New Revised Standard Version) is one of the more accessible and accurate translations of the Old Testament/Hebrew Scriptures. The reader is encouraged to have the *NRSV* beside them, to read the prophetic passages and texts themselves as they read the chapters of this book. Sometimes a prophetic text is quoted in the book; at other times a reference to a text is given.

The term *Israel* is used in two senses throughout the book. The word is used as a general descriptor for the community addressed by the prophets (*Amos* 4:12). In this sense the word is used in a religious sense, identifying a group distinguished from other countries in the ANE (Ancient Near East) not only by political boundaries but more importantly by religious history and affiliation. The word Israel is also used in the more technical sense as the name of the northern kingdom (with its capital Samaria), the venue of the prophetic ministries of Amos and Hosea, as opposed to the southern kingdom or kingdom of Judah (with its capital Jerusalem).

In the Christian tradition prophecy represents one of the great bridges between the Old Testament and the New Testament. Jesus is presented as modelling and fulfilling a prophetic role (*Luke* 4:16-30). The New Testament writers recognise and signal the role of prophecy in appreciating the life and ministry of Jesus of Nazareth in their use of the mantra "this happened in fulfilment of the scriptures" (*Luke* 4:21; *John* 19:36-37). The prophetic literature appears in both the Hebrew canon and the Christian canon as inspired literature, as sacred to both monotheistic faiths. Use is made of BCE in this book to indicate dates in recognition of the pivotal interpretive role prophecy played in the formation of both the Hebrew and Christian canons.

The prophetic literature in the Old Testament/Hebrew Scriptures is inspired literature. It is the literary product of both human and divine authors. It has a character, then, which distinguishes it from comparative prophetic literature of other ANE nations. The Nicene Creed identifies this key character and authorship: "I believe in the Holy Spirit, the Lord and giver of life ... who has spoken through the prophets."

Brian Boyle

Jesus is presented as modelling and fulfilling a prophetic role (Luke 4:16-30). The New Testament writers recognise and signal the role of prophecy in appreciating the life and ministry of Jesus of Nazareth in their use of the mantra "this happened in fulfilment of the scriptures."
(Luke 4:21; John 19:36-37)

Introduction

Prophecy was not about foretelling the future. The prophets were more interested in the present, in changing people's behaviour and perceptions "now", than in predicting the future.

left: fresco of prophets Isaiah, Jeremiah, Ezekiel and Daniel

We can begin by asking some fundamental questions: why read the prophets of ancient Israel today? What relevance do they have for us? What can we learn from them? The purpose of this book is to offer the general reader an introduction to the fascinating phenomenon of prophecy in Israel, as we find it in the Bible. The prophetic movement spanned approximately three hundred years, between the eighth and fifth centuries before Christ. It had a vital and enduring impact on Israel's religion and faith. We read the prophets today for basically three reasons: the prophets were fascinating and engaging individuals themselves; the world they lived and ministered in, with all its social, political and religious aspects, was a world rather similar to our own; and, finally, the prophets reveal a great deal to us about relationship with God and with each other. The prophets offer us an enduring legacy. This book aims to demonstrate their relevance and to encourage the general reader to pick up something of the fire of these extraordinary people by reading the texts.

While the prophetic movement in Israel had many features common to each of the prophets contained in the canon of scripture, prophecy was also a varied phenomenon. Each prophet, for example, needs to be situated within his specific religious, social and political context to understand his ministry and preaching. No two prophets were necessarily the same. Jeremiah and Ezekiel were contemporaries, active at the time of the first siege of Jerusalem in 597 BCE, but their messages were somewhat different. Only some of the principal prophets of Israel are presented here (Amos, Hosea, Isaiah, Jeremiah and Ezekiel) and again only selections from their preaching and oracles are examined here. The purpose of the book is to introduce the reader to the phenomenon of prophecy by examining some of its key proponents. This book is intended to be a sampler, to encourage the reader to read more of the prophetic texts.

It is probably easier to say what prophecy in Israel was not, rather than to say positively what this varied and fascinating phenomenon was. Further, prophecy was not anti-religion. Many of the great prophets (Isaiah, Jeremiah and Ezekiel) were priests themselves. The prophets did not set about destroying Israel's religious cult; rather, their purpose was to bring it back to its authentic holiness, to enable the cult to rediscover its capacity to make people holy. Prophecy and religion went hand in hand. Certainly, the prophets found themselves in conflict with religious institutions as they claimed a direct authority from God for their preaching (*Amos* 7:10-17) rather than an authority mediated through the cult. Stated positively, the prophets were first and foremost *intercessors* between God and the community, messengers of the Lord. The greatest, and most successful, of all intercessors was Moses (*Deuteronomy* 34:10-12). All prophets are presented as modelled on Moses, particularly in the call narratives of the prophets (*Isaiah* 6:1-13; *Jeremiah* 1:4-19). The prophets were inspired, engaging, charismatic individuals whose message to ancient Israel is still relevant and inspiring for contemporary readers and believers.

Israel's first kings

When the twelve tribes eventually settled in Palestine (the promised land) after the Exodus from Egypt under the leadership of Moses and the forty years wandering in the Sinai desert, the people quickly became aware that their political survival in the new land depended on unity among themselves and strong leadership. The tribes were faced by powerful kingdoms on the Mediterranean seaboard and in the areas east of the Jordan river. In seeking unity and leadership the tribes eventually opted for the form of government common in the Ancient Near East: monarchy. The first king of the united Israel was **Saul** (1020-1000 BCE), from the tribe of Benjamin, the weakest of the tribes. This was a strategic choice: a king from the smallest tribe posed no threat to the stronger tribes. Saul was a charismatic leader and a great military general. Saul, however, fell out of favour with God and was eventually replaced as king by **David** (1000-961 BCE), but only after a protracted and bitter civil war. David was the archetypal king in Israel. He enjoyed God's favour and support (see *2 Samuel* 7). David was succeeded as king by his son **Solomon** (961-922 BCE), famous for his wisdom and the sophistication of his court. The empire of David and Solomon represented the highpoint of Israel's military power in the region. With the death of Solomon, however, and the succession of his son Rehoboam (922-915 BCE) the great Davidic empire divided into two separate kingdoms: the kingdom of Israel (or the northern kingdom) with its capital Samaria and the kingdom of Judah (or southern kingdom) with its capital Jerusalem. While related in origins the two kingdoms had a tense rivalry. The kingdom of Israel lasted until 722 BCE when it was absorbed into the Assyrian empire as provinces and ceased to exist as a political entity. The kingdom of Judah lasted until 587 BCE when it

King David

was conquered by the Babylonian emperor Nebuchadnezzar. Jerusalem was burnt, the Temple destroyed, and the last Davidic king was taken into exile in Babylon. The southern kingdom too ceased to exist as a political entity.

Prophets and kings

It is important to sketch out this brief history of monarchy in Israel to better understand the emergence of the prophetic movement since the prophets were in frequent confrontation with the kings. Their relationship was often tense and abrasive. Prophecy was, by its very nature, a charismatic phenomenon. It was not institutional and did not operate on a succession basis, but derived its authority from the prophet's call by God and not from political power. Monarchy, on the other hand, was an institution sanctioned by God and based on power and succession. Such forces inevitably were in conflict. Prophets were not opposed to monarchy as such. Rather, the prophets tended to criticise the kings for their failure to establish justice and righteousness in the kingdom, seen as the primary duty of kings (see *Jeremiah* 22:13-19), while the kings tended to see prophets as troublemakers (see *1 Kings* 18:16-19). This fraught relationship between prophet and king provided much of the energy for prophetic activity. To understand the prophetic movement and to understand each prophet we need to see the tense relationship between prophecy and monarchy in general and the relationship between an individual prophet and king in particular at any given time.

The emergence of prophecy

Prophecy in Israel did not simply come from nowhere or fall down from heaven. It emerged at a particular time in history and endured centre stage for several centuries because two key factors came together powerfully in Israel's history: the significant socio-economic change brought about by the shift from an agricultural and subsistence based economy to a more commercial and mercantile economy and the consequent impact on a poor population; and secondly, the aggressive expansion into Israel's territory by its superpower neighbours in the north. We can briefly examine each of these two key factors.

KINGS OF THE UNITED ISRAEL
Saul 1020-1000 BCE (approx.)
David 1000-961 BCE (approx.)
Solomon 961-922 BCE (approx.)
Division of the kingdom with the death of Solomon

KINGDOM OF ISRAEL (922-722/721 BCE) Northern Kingdom (Samaria)		PROPHETS	KINGDOM OF JUDAH (922-587 BCE) Southern Kingdom (Jerusalem)	
Jeroboam I	922-901		Rehoboam	922-915
Omri	876-869		Jehoshaphat	873-849
Ahab	869-850	Elijah	Joash	837-800
Jehoram	849-842	Elisha	Amaziah	800-783
Jehu	842-815			
Jeroboam II	786-746	Amos	Uzziah	783-742
		Hosea		
Hoshea	732-724	Isaiah	Ahaz	732-715
		Micah		

Fall of the Kingdom of Israel and its incorporation into the Assyrian empire 722/721 BCE.

		Isaiah	Hezekiah	715-686
			Manasseh	686-642
		Zephaniah	Jehoshaphat	873-849
		Jeremiah	Josiah	640-609
		Nahum	Jehoahaz	609
		Habakkuk	Jehoiakim	609-598
			Jehoiachin	597
		Ezekiel	Zedekiah	597-587

First Babylonian siege of Jerusalem 597 BCE
Second Babylonian siege of Jerusalem, capture and destruction of the city 588-587 BCE
Babylonian exile 587/6-539 BCE

left: timeline of reigns of kings and key prophets

Social and economic changes

The changes in the socio-economic profile of the state were largely set in train by the policies of Solomon and his successors. While some benefited from the new wealth, many did not. These changes effectively introduced a structural violence into society: a new moneyed class able to use the laws of credit and property inheritance to their financial interest, and a new underclass who were ruthlessly exploited and denied their rights in credit arrangements, property ownership and inheritance, and representation before the law. Effectively, there was no solidarity. The poor became chattel, to be bought and sold (see *Amos* 2:6-8). We can take a good example from Israel's history of how monarchy and prophecy clashed in the emergence of this new society. Jeroboam II was king in Israel (northern kingdom) for some forty years (786-746 BCE). His counterpart in Judah (southern kingdom) was Uzziah who also reigned for these forty years (783-742 BCE).

For both kingdoms these were times of ostensible wealth, security and peace. However, as the prophet **Amos** persistently pointed out: this wealth was being achieved at considerable social cost to a hidden and voiceless underclass. The question was: at what social cost has this prosperity been achieved? Amos, as God's champion, spoke up for the poor. **Hosea**, as his contemporary, had a similar message. God does indeed have favourites and is on the side of the poor.

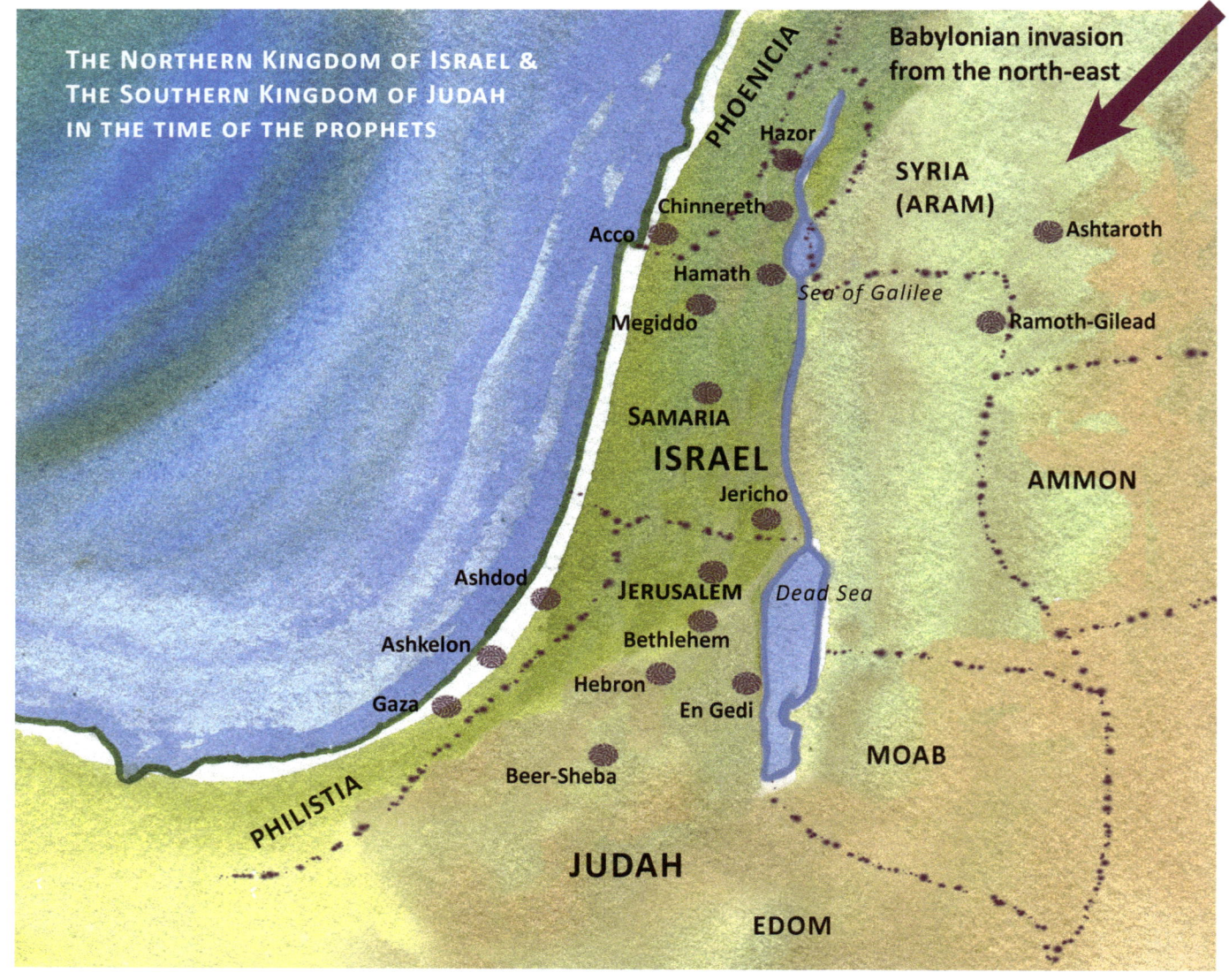

The Northern Kingdom of Israel & The Southern Kingdom of Judah in the time of the prophets

Dealing with superpowers

The second key factor for the emergence of the prophetic movement in Israel in the eighth century was the considerable political instability brought about by the aggressive expansionist policies of the Assyrian empire to the north firstly and then by the Babylonian empire as their successors. Over several hundred years from the times of **Amos** and **Hosea** to the times of **Jeremiah** and **Ezekiel** the small petty kingdoms of Israel and Judah endured persistent political and strategic instability at the hands of their superpower neighbours. The only way to survive was to enter into strategic alliance as a vassal state. The prophets were not opposed to the necessity of such alliance making; rather, their concern was that God was being persistently left out of the equation. Prophets like Amos and Hosea were making the point that God as the sovereign lord of history was at work in history to bring about the divine purposes. The appearance of the Assyrians at the city gates was not just simply a strategic occurrence; God had brought the Assyrians to the gates as the instruments of divine justice! Again, we can take an example from Israel's history to illustrate this key factor facilitating the rise of prophecy. **Isaiah** was prophet in Jerusalem during the reigns of Ahaz (732-715 BCE) and Hezekiah (715-686 BCE) at a time when Assyria was menacing the kingdom of Judah. The northern kingdom was absorbed into the Assyrian empire at this time (722 BCE). Isaiah urged Ahaz to have faith in God's promises (see *Isaiah* 7:1-9) when his kingdom was under threat. Ahaz preferred to hedge his bets. Isaiah was inviting him to carefully discern the divine purposes in these threatened times. Similarly, a century later, Jeremiah urged the last Davidic king in Judah, Zedekiah (597-587 BCE), to listen to the voice of the Lord in dire times of the Babylonian siege of Jerusalem and have faith (see *Jeremiah* 38:14-26). However, political expediency or cowardice prevailed and the city was destroyed (587-586 BCE). Prophecy then emerged in times of political uncertainty as a clear and alternate voice to military power.

The message of the prophets

The message of the prophets could be summarised under several key points. Firstly, given the socio-economic changes to Israelite society and the emergence of the new rich commercial class, there was no sense of solidarity with the marginalised. The new society had created a vast number of hidden poor who had no voice. These persons were being ignored. Secondly, the kings of Israel and Judah relied unduly on political alliances and strategic arrangements to survive politically. The prophets challenged the kings to have faith in God as the lord of history. Further, these same kings were failing in their essential duty of establishing justice in the kingdom, especially for the poor. Thirdly, the prophets often criticised the official religious cult as being an obstacle to faith rather than promoting faith. The prophets were not anti-religion or anti-cult but rather critical of

> *Prophecy then emerged in times of political uncertainty as a clear and alternate voice to military power.*

the compromises cult had made to gain power and wealth. Amos was savage in his criticism of the cult of his day (*Amos* 4:4-5). We could say then that the prophets offered a complete challenge to their societies: political, social and religious aspects. However, they were not revolutionaries or social reformers. The prophet's task was to see clearly (from God's perspective) what needed to be done; they left the task of renewal or reform to others. Prophets were involved in the present, rather than the future. They were more interested in bringing God's word to their contemporaries than in predicting the future. They wanted people to see what was really going on, beyond surface appearances. For the prophets a people that has no idea of its present has no future. Hosea expressed the matter well: "a people without understanding comes to ruin" (4:14).

CHAPTER ONE

Israel's Prophets

Who were the prophets?

In considering the question, who were the prophets in Israel, we could make several key general statements, before looking at the specific features that characterised the prophet. The phenomenon of prophecy emerged in Israel around the eighth century before Christ with the prophets Elijah and Elisha, and remained a potent force in Israel's life well into the time of the Babylonian exile in the sixth century and afterwards. Prophecy then was a key phenomenon in Israel's life over several centuries. We also note that prophecy was directly related to the institution of monarchy. The prophets tended to be trenchant critics of the kings mainly because of the failure of these rulers to bring about social justice in society. While prophets were respected, or at least tolerated, the relationship between prophets and kings was usually a tense one.

The prophets were divinely inspired in their messages. Kings could not claim the same divine inspiration. The problem with prophecy was that prophets did not claim or need the

> *Surely the Lord God does nothing, without revealing his secret to his servants the prophets. The lion has roared; who will not fear? The Lord God has spoken; who can but prophesy?*
>
> Amos 3: 7-8

authority of any human institution, whether monarchy or religious cult, to validate their message. The prophet had a direct relationship with God and did not need an intermediary. While not necessarily anti-monarchy or anti-cult in terms of Israel's religion and faith, prophets did not need to look to human institutions for authority or support. The prophetic claim was the claim to know the truth, inspired by God. While the prophet was sure of the source or origin of his inspiration and (generally) sure of his message, the problem for the prophet was to convince his target audience that his was indeed an authentic message from the Lord. Prophecy as a charismatic phenomenon oftentimes found itself in conflict with institutional authority, whether political or religious, precisely because its claim to the truth lay outside the validating processes of human authority.

So, who were these fascinating individuals, the prophets of Israel, and how could we begin to outline the key and essential features which marked this person as "a prophet". We could say a prophet in Israel was a person characterised by the following features:

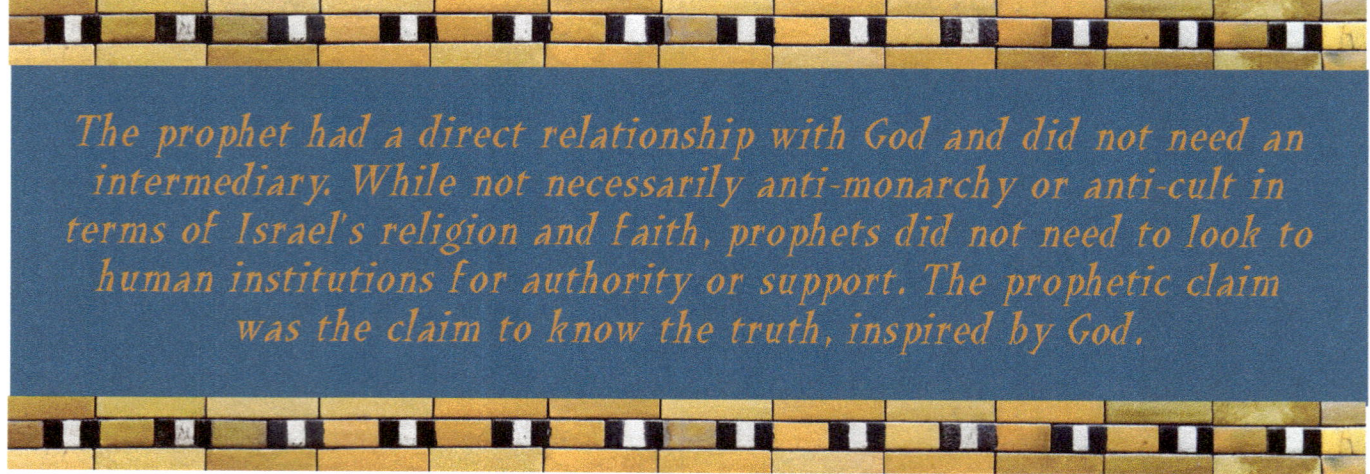

The prophet had a direct relationship with God and did not need an intermediary. While not necessarily anti-monarchy or anti-cult in terms of Israel's religion and faith, prophets did not need to look to human institutions for authority or support. The prophetic claim was the claim to know the truth, inspired by God.

Features of a prophet

- **Someone who was called and commissioned by God.** This divine commissioning was a basic sign of authenticity. We find several call narratives in the prophetic books (*Jeremiah* 1, *Isaiah* 6, *Ezekiel* 1-3). The call narrative validated the community's belief that this person was called by God. The prophet is a person who has received and delivered a message from the Lord.

- **The prophet was modelled after the role of Moses.** In the *Book of Deuteronomy* there are two keypassages (18:15; 34:10-12) which speak of the unique position and authority of Moses. He is presented as the archetypal prophet. All prophets must be modelled after Moses.

- **Like Moses, the prophet was fundamentally an intercessor.** The key role or task of Moses as described in the *Books of Exodus, Leviticus, Numbers* and *Deuteronomy* was to be an intercessor before God on behalf of the people. Moses was a very successful intercessor. This same task of intercession was a key one for the prophets (*Jeremiah* 42:1-6).

- **The prophets were persons of a heart-felt trust in the Lord and persons of moral-earnestness (McKane).** The prophets were persons who had a strong, personal relationship with the Lord, persons whom, in our culture, we might describe as saints. Trust and fidelity were key in this relationship. They were also persons of a finely-tuned conscience, of moral sensibility. They clearly identified right from wrong (in a society which tended to cloud or merge these distinctions) and had a passion for justice.

- **The prophets were inspired and charismatic individuals.** Because their authority came directly from their personal relationship with God, the prophets had no need for the validation or approval of human authority. Indeed, true prophets oftentimes found themselves in conflict with hereditary monarchy and religious cult. Prophets were exceptional individuals.

- **Every prophet came from a specific social and geo-political context.** While prophecy had an identifiable form and characteristics, there was no such thing as one size fits all. Each prophet needs to be situated and read within the particular circumstances of his ministry, the prevailing social and religious issues of the time, and the wider geo-political context of the Ancient Near East. To give one illustration: Jeremiah and Ezekiel were contemporaries (whether they met or knew each other is another interesting question) and both were prophets at the time of the fall of Jerusalem to the Babylonian armies in 587 BCE and the subsequent exile. The nature of their message and the immediate circumstances which shaped their respective ministries, however, were not necessarily the same.

- **Prophets were concerned with exhortation, rather than prediction, with the present, rather than the future.** Prophecy was not about foretelling the future. Some prophets did engage in foretelling the future, with varied success. Prophets were more interested in exhorting their audience to a change of heart and a change of lifestyle now rather than predicting the future. Prophets were focussed on the present, rather than the future.

- **Prophets were persons of vital, emotional preaching (Blenkinsopp).** Prophecy involved public performance. The prophet was required to speak and to act in public. Prophecy was not for the faint hearted or the introverted. The prophet had to deliver his message or act out a pantomime in a public square or at the city gate. The prophet, then, had to convince his target audience of the authenticity of his message and the need for them to act on that message. Prophets had to be good salesmen!

- **Prophets were preachers of repentance.** Prophecy worked on the basis that the prophet had an authentic insight into the true nature of his own society. The prophet's task was to expose the (hidden) underbelly of his society, the ways in which prosperity and peace may have been achieved at the social cost of poorer members of society. The prophet was a person with a keen vision, who could see things as they really were. His task was to call people to repentance. Outward prosperity and wealth were not true indicators of divine favour nor indicators that everything was well with society.

🔲 **Prophets used words, actions, gestures, even silence.** Prophets spoke the word of the Lord. Much of their prophetic ministry then was about speaking and about public performance. However, prophecy was more than words. Prophets were called upon by the Lord to perform symbolic actions and to engage in pantomines as the proclamation of the word. At times a prophet could also use silence as the word of the Lord. Silence was not the absence of the prophetic word, but the word of the Lord in that form.

🔲 **The Prophets called Israel to holiness.** The prophet's task was to call Israel back to holiness of life since holiness was the distinguishing feature of God. Repentance restored holiness. The prophets understood holiness to mean monotheistic faith (belief in the one God) and covenant relationship (fidelity to the Mosaic covenant).

🔲 **Prophets drew on the genius of Israel's faith.** Prophecy endured so long at the centre of Israel's life and had such a profound effect on society because it essentially drew on and appealed to the enduring values of that faith. These values included covenant fidelity and monotheistic belief. The prophets of Israel did not invent a religious system or a new faith. The prophets appealed to the genius of the faith already there. Their task was to restore that genius to the centre of Israel's life through repentance and the call to holiness in behaviour.

🔲 **The prophets were not anti-religion or anti-cult.** The prophets were not opposed to religion and religious cult as such. Indeed, prophets such as Isaiah, Jeremiah and Ezekiel were priests themselves. What the prophets opposed was a religion and a cult that had become corrupt and that had permitted itself to become a state-sponsored institution. Prophets such as Isaiah and Ezekiel had an exquisite sense of the beauty of the holy and of holy things and were not opposed to the cult. They were not the world's first liberal protestants. The prophets would have delighted in the religious aesthetics of our liturgies and been at home in our cathedrals. For them, one could have justice and beauty.

🔲 **Prophets either instigated or inspired literary traditions.** There is good evidence in the prophetic literature that prophets such as Jeremiah and Ezekiel wrote, composed and edited material and oracles found in the books which bear their name (*Jeremiah* 36:1-32). Prophets such as Amos and Hosea may well have gathered groups of disciples around them who collected and edited their oracles. The canonical prophets each inspired the literary tradition named after them.

🔲 **Prophets were heroic and tragic figures (Wellhausen), alienated from their communities.** Generally, prophets were not popular figures. Popularity could tend to be a sign of false prophecy. People were wary, guarded about the prophet since the message was not always welcome (doom and gloom) and one could not always be sure the prophet was authentic. Being a prophet involved heroism since the ministry brought suspicion, alienation and hostility from people. The prophet had to be his own man.

🔲 **The God of the prophets was a God who is holy, righteous and merciful (Kuenen).** Born of their own intense and personal relationship with the Lord, the God of the prophets had these three distinguishing features. *God is firstly holy*. Divine holiness sanctifies every person and everything which comes within its ambit. Israel is called to be holy as God is holy. *God is righteous*. The test of a correct faith relationship with God is not (necessarily) ritual and piety, but rather commitment to social justice. Righteousness is evident in attention to those who have fallen through the cracks of society. *God is merciful*. The God of the prophets is a God who is long-suffering and patient, a God who can be appealed to through intercession. The prophets were aware that the message of rep entance they preached was a message addressed to themselves in the first instance. The God they had encountered in their own lives was the holy, righteous and merciful God they preached to their contemporaries.

When and why did prophecy emerge in Israel?

With the emergence of the prophets Amos, Hosea, Micah and Isaiah in the eighth century, prophecy in Israel assumed some distinctive features. There were certainly other prophets in Israel before these individuals, prophets like Samuel, Elijah and Elisha; however, with the emergence of Amos and others we might say the *classical* form of prophecy became apparent, with three distinctive features in particular: high level of literary skill, capacity to interpret the wider geo-political situation in the Ancient Near East, and a comprehensive challenge to Israelite society as a whole. Let us look at each of these features of classic prophecy.

Most persons in ancient Israel were illiterate. Literacy was the skill of only a few people, among whom we find our classical prophets. Literacy meant not just simply some form of education but also acumen, insight and capacity to make judgements about the world and their society. Prophets were insightful individuals. Their prophetic message, delivered in oracles, was written down and preserved, either by the prophet himself or by his school of followers and disciples. The message was seen as relevant, not simply for their own time but for future generations, and hence it was committed to writing. With Samuel, Elijah and Elisha we have stories and narratives *about* the prophets; with Amos, Hosea and Isaiah we have the *substance* of their preaching and teaching.

We note secondly that prophets like Amos situate their preaching within a wide geo-political context. We might say they internationalise their message. They are not concerned simply with the local and national impact of their preaching in Israel but they see their message in the wider stage of international politics in the Ancient Near East. In the geo-political and geo-strategic movements and clashes of the three great superpowers of the time (Assyria, Babylon, Egypt) these prophets see not just the fate of a small state like Israel being effected or determined, but the hand of God in these events. God is the lord of history. Everything occurs and unfolds according to the divine will. God is working in the events of the international arena to bring about the divine purpose. The prophets discern a theological meaning in the geo-political events of their time and the impact of these events on Israel. They invite their contemporaries, their target audiences, to reflect on these events and consider these changes, particularly in terms of Israel's covenant relationship with the Lord.

A third distinctive feature of the prophetic careers of Amos, Hosea and others was the comprehensive challenge they offered to their societies as a whole, not just simply religious but social and economic challenge as well. They did not compartmentalise faith and religion away from the socio-economic features of society. The litmus test of true faith and religion was not (necessarily) piety but commitment to justice. Economic prosperity, whether national or individual, was not (necessarily) an indication of divine favour or approval. Similarly, peace and social stability did not (necessarily) indicate that society in general was in right covenant relationship with the Lord. The prophetic challenge was simply: at what social and economic cost to the poorer members of society has this prosperity been achieved? The prophets were interested in the comprehensive impact of their prophetic word on society in all its religious, social and economic forms.

Two factors in particular in eighth century Israel aided the emergence and growth of the prophetic movement and ensured it played a central role: the significant change in what we might call the socio-economic profile of society, and the aggressive expansion of Assyrian military power into this part of the world. Again, let us consider each of these two factors since they give us a good indication as to why prophecy was so important and played such a central role in Israel's life and faith.

In the time after the death of King Solomon (c. 922 BCE) and the subsequent division of the Davidic empire into the two kingdoms of

Israel (northern kingdom) and Judah (southern kingdom), we might say that Israelite society underwent a significant socio-economic change with the shift from a largely agricultural society to a more mercantile economy base. Broadly speaking this shift meant the rise of a commercial class, consolidation of land holdings and emergence of international trade. While these changes brought prosperity to many in society, they also created a significant underclass, often hidden or simply ignored. These persons became the subject of prophetic preaching. Prophets like Amos identified a structural violence in society. There was no solidarity. The poor were not seen as persons needing economic and social assistance but as goods to be bought and sold for profit. The poor were those who were exploited, against whom the rich and powerful could use laws of credit to their advantage. The poor were those disenfranchised from their ancestral lands and in extreme cases sold into slavery for payment of debts. Prophets like Amos offered an articulate, comprehensive challenge to their society: God is not blind to this inequality, God is not impartial, God is on the side of the poor. The significant socio-economic changes in Israelite society then aided the emergence and growth of the prophetic movement.

A second factor for this growth was the rise of Assyria in the eighth century as the dominant superpower in the north. The Assyrian armies pushed aggressively into Syria and Palestine. They represented a potent and ever present military threat to Israel. Eventually, at the time of the prophets Amos and Hosea, the northern kingdom of Israel was absorbed into the Assyrian empire as provinces and ceased to exist as a political entity (722 BCE). The survival of the southern kingdom of Judah with its capital Jerusalem was precarious for the next 150 years. The expansion of the Assyrian juggernaut brought with it shifting military alliances as Judah attempted to simply survive, constant external threat, payment of massive tribute, and the inability of Judah's kings to skilfully and astutely read the political signs of their times. Prophets like Amos and Hosea saw in this military expansion not simply the quest for hegemony by the Assyrians but the hand of the Lord. God was working through these events to bring about the divine purposes for Israel and Judah. Infidelity to God had political consequences. The unstable and threatening geo-political situation in which Israel found itself in the face of Assyrian power became a ready context in which prophecy might assume a central role. Prophets like Amos, Hosea, Micah and Isaiah formed a religious opposition to the socio-economic exploitation and the political manoeuvring of the times.

Adapted from: Rainer Albertz, *A History of Israelite Religion in the Old Testament Period: volume 1: from the beginnings to the end of the monarchy.* London: SCM Press, 1994, 156-163.

What did prophets preach about?

While each of the prophets has to be situated within their specific social and cultural context and no two prophets were the same, we could say that there were common themes or concerns in their preaching, and we can identify four such concerns here.

Firstly, the prophets were concerned about the inherent injustice in society and the lack of any sense of solidarity with the marginalised, those who had slipped through the cracks. This injustice was evident in the social profile: loss of ancestral lands and the rise of large commercial estates, growing numbers of rural poor, recourse to law courts and the use of debt laws by the rich and influential at the expense of the poor and the insensitive lifestyle of the rich. These social inequalities were glaring to men like Amos, Hosea and Isaiah but largely ignored by those who profited from this exploitation.

above: King Ashurnasirpal

Secondly, the prophets criticised the military alliances of the kings of Israel and Judah and the system of shifting loyalties such alliances necessarily created. The prophets were not against armies or military power as such, nor critical of the need of a small kingdom like Judah to effectively seek survival by alliance. What the prophets criticised was undue reliance on powerful neighbours at the neglect of relationship with the Lord. The prophets were clear: Israel's victories were not (necessarily) God's victories, Israel's defeats were not (necessarily) God's defeats. Fidelity, truth and loyalty need to be evident in alliances.

Thirdly, the prophets tended to be trenchant critics of the monarchs. Elijah was a vocal opponent and strong critic of King Ahab. In the northern kingdom particularly dynastic succession and change of dynasty were often accompanied by violent bloodshed. The principal task of the king in Israel was to effectively ensure justice in society. With few exceptions (Hezekiah, Josiah), the prophets were inclined to condemn the kings for their uniform failure to bring about justice for all in society.

Fourthly, the prophets tended to be critical of the religious cult and worship. Again, the prophets were not anti-religion or anti-cult. Several of the prophets (Jeremiah, Isaiah and Ezekiel) were priests themselves and had a native sympathy for the cult as the worship of God and for the aesthetics of worship. What prophets vociferously opposed and condemned was a cult which had become fatally flawed. These flaws were evident, for example, in widespread syncretism in worship, that is, where pagan elements had been incorporated into the worship of the Lord. Monotheistic faith had become compromised by the addition or absorption of pagan practices into Temple cult. People could not see the harm in this practice. The value of true religion was being insidiously undermined by such practices. Religion was bankrupt. The prophets called for a cleansing, both institutional and personal. There was radical need for deep reflection on the state of the religious cult and relationship with God.

Adapted from: Rainer Albertz, *A History of Israelite Religion in the Old Testament Period: volume 1: from the beginnings to the end of the monarchy,* 163-186.

How can you tell if prophecy is true?

One of the greatest challenges the audiences whom the prophets addressed had to face was the question: is this an authentic word from the Lord? How can we know if this prophecy is true? In a bewildering array of prophets in ancient Israel the issue of determining true prophecy from false prophecy was a difficult one, even for a prophet. There were many prophets in ancient Israel and most were false prophets who misled people with fake assurances of peace and security. The prophets we have in the Bible now are what we call canonical prophets, that is, the believing community has come to the sure conviction that persons like Amos, Hosea and Isaiah were truly inspired by the Lord and were true prophets. However, that judgement has only come after a long period of time, and generally after the death of the true prophet. Understandably, audiences were suspicious, and especially when the message preached was unwelcome and unpalatable. So, how did people determine true prophecy from false prophecy?

The *Book of Deuteronomy* (18:15-22) offers several criteria for determining authentic prophecy. Firstly, the prophet must be a prophet like Moses, the archetypal prophet. The prophet's preaching must be consistent with the message Moses preached. Secondly, the message preached must be consistent with monotheistic faith, that is, a prophet who preaches any other god apart from the Lord is a false prophet. Thirdly, the source of the prophetic word must be the Lord, that is, the call and commission to preach comes from God. The prophet who preaches on the basis of his own (perceived) commission is a false prophet. Fourthly, if a matter prophesied does not take place or is not proved true, this is presumptive and false prophecy.

It is easy to see, however, that these criteria are not totally satisfactory as some relate to predictive prophecy, that is foretelling the future, and others appear to beg the question. Predicting the future was not a principal prophetic activity. Prophets were more interested in the present than in the future. Besides, the community may have to wait a long time for a prediction to pass, sometimes beyond the lifetime of the prophet. It was relatively easy to see whether a prophet's preaching was consistent with monotheistic faith. However, how could you tell whether the prophet had actually been commissioned by God or not? The community is faced with a difficult and perplexing issue. Ultimately it becomes a matter of discernment and reflection. Prophets like Jeremiah and Isaiah are canonical prophets because the believing community has come to the considered judgment that they were true prophets, oftentimes over a long period of time.

Jesus as prophet

There are at least two places in the New Testament where Jesus is identified as a prophet by others or where his preaching and actions lead people to believe that he is a prophet. The first of these is Luke's account of the inaugural homily of Jesus in the synagogue of Nazareth, his home town (*Luke* 4:14-30). Jesus' reputation as a preacher and miracle worker in the other lakeside towns has preceded his return to his own town. The people have great expectations of him. They want impressive teaching and miracles. They see his preaching and teaching as modelling and fulfilling the role of a prophet, like the prophets of old. In the popular imagination Jesus too is a prophet. He teaches with authority like the prophets did. However, Jesus does not claim this title of prophet for himself. In fact he disabuses them of the expectations they have about him. He recognises that his role is to teach, to preach and to work miracles but he is wary of the title "prophet".

The second text is also from Luke. It is the famous story of the post-resurrection appearance of Jesus to the disciples on the road to Emmaus (*Luke* 24:1-35). The two disciples are discouraged and downhearted because Jesus has been crucified. Their hopes for him have been seemingly dashed. When Jesus walks with them as a stranger they tell him that their hopes had been that Jesus was a prophet "mighty in deed and word before God and all the people" (verse 19). Like the people in the earlier story in the Nazareth synagogue, these two disciples associate Jesus' actions and deeds with those of the prophets of old. For them Jesus is a prophet, although a failed one now! Again, Jesus focuses on the activity of preaching and teaching but not on the title of "prophet". He draws the attention of the disciples to the fulfilment of the scriptures and particularly through his suffering and death (verses 25-27). They recognise him eventually in the breaking of bread at the simple evening meal (verses 30-32). Full of joy they return to Jerusalem that evening to share the good news.

Jesus did not call himself a prophet. The New Testament writers, however, are keen to say two things about Jesus as a prophet: firstly, that in his life, ministry, suffering, death and resurrection Jesus has fulfilled all the prophecies of the sacred scriptures. Secondly, Jesus is greater than the prophets and particularly greater than the prophet Moses. In the sermon on the mount discourse, for example, Matthew presents Jesus not just as a new Moses but as one who surpasses Moses in teaching authority (see *Matthew* 5:1-48). At the transfiguration of Jesus (*Luke* 9:28-36) Moses (representing the law) and Elijah (representing prophecy) appear with the glorified Christ and are depicted as being in conversation with him. Law and prophecy in the sacred scriptures bear witness to Jesus. He fulfils these prophecies but he is more than simply another prophet.

We could say that prophecy and the fulfilment of prophecy is the principal bridge between the Old Testament and the New Testament. The Gospel writers want to present Jesus as fulfilling the prophecies of old and they will do this thematically and stylistically by linking a prophecy of old with an action of Jesus. For example, in the Nazareth synagogue story Luke has Jesus quote directly from the prophecy of Isaiah (*Isaiah* 61:1-2) in his homily, bringing good news to the poor and comfort to the weary, indicating this prophecy is being fulfilled as he speaks. Another example is found at the death of Jesus where John links the crucified body of Jesus on the cross with a prophecy in the Psalms (*John* 19:24 and *Psalm* 22:18), showing how this prophecy has also been fulfilled: not one of his bones will be broken. There are many other such examples in the Gospels. The New Testament writers then want to present Jesus as the greatest of prophets, mighty in word and deed before God and the people. They do this principally by showing how Jesus fulfilled the words of the prophets in his own words and deeds. Prophecy then becomes the bridge linking the two testaments of the Christian bible.

SUMMARY

- Prophets were persons with literary skills and education.
- Prophetic message needs to be situated in the wider political context.
- Prophets offered a comprehensive challenge to their society.
- The change in socio-economic profile in ancient Israel facilitated the rise of prophecy.
- Likewise, the rise of superpowers like Assyria gave the prophetic message some urgency.

CHAPTER TWO

Amos

A ROARING LION

Prophet
  Amos
Description
  Social critic
Occupation
  Sheep breeder and agriculturalist
Time of ministry
  Eighth century BCE
Place of ministry
  Northern Kingdom of Israel
Message
  Condemns luxurious and insensitive lifestyle of the rich at a time of widespread social need, demonstrating a lack of solidarity in society.

> *But let justice roll down like waters, and righteousness like an ever flowing stream.*
> Amos 5:24

The prophet Amos and the socio-economic context of his preaching

Amos was a shepherd and livestock breeder from Tekoa, in the southern kingdom of Judah (1:1; 7:14), called by the Lord to a prophetic ministry in the northern kingdom of Israel. His ministry coincided with the reigns of Jeroboam II (786-746 BCE) in Israel and Uzziah (783-742 BCE) in Judah. Both of these kings enjoyed long reigns (unusual for the times) in which there was relative peace, political stability and economic prosperity in both kingdoms. People tended to see the stability and prosperity of these reigns as indicators of divine approval. Amos assumed a counter stance. Bethel, the royal sanctuary in the northern kingdom, was the *locus* and place of some of this defiant preaching (7:12). His prophetic oracles which have come down to us now in the canonical *Book of Amos* have been edited by his disciples in the southern kingdom, and so reflect the perspective of that kingdom. Amos prophesied the destruction of the northern kingdom (7:11) with attendant exile and deportation for sections of the community (which came to pass in 722 BCE) at a time when such a threat from Assyria in the north was not obviously apparent. His prophetic career may have been a short one, returning afterwards to his trade.

A snapshot of the prophet

What we can know about Amos, his prophetic career and how he himself understood his calling from the Lord is contained in the famous dispute or confrontation between Amos and the priest Amaziah at the Bethel sanctuary of the northern kingdom. The incident is recounted in the *Book of Amos,* 7:10-17. The priest Amaziah challenges Amos' right to prophesy and basically says he should go home! Amos' preaching is not welcome and is not politically correct. Amos gives the priest Amaziah a fiery response saying he did not belong to any of the prophetic brotherhoods, was simply a shepherd and herdsman, but had been called by God to prophesy in Israel (7:14-15). He announces the dissolution of the northern kingdom and deportation in exile, as well as personal misfortune for Amaziah and his family. We see in this confrontation features of Amos' style of preaching: an abrasive, confrontational style with a focus on a powerful social critique. Amos would have made few friends in the northern kingdom! We note also in this confrontation how Amos dissociates himself from conventional and acceptable prophetic activity and establishes his authority for his mission in his call from the Lord (7:15). This call to be prophet has been insistent in his life (3:8). Here is a man out of step with his times, but one who has a keen insight and understanding of the true nature of his society.

Amos perceptively identifies the problem in Israel and its cause. He sees a lack of justice in society and a lack of righteousness in people's lives, evident in such widespread practices as debt slavery, seizure of property, seizure of pledges held as collateral for loans and sexual immorality (3:9-4:3; 5:10-13). This is a society without a sense of solidarity. Corruption in the courts is endemic. What is worse the demoralised are silent (5:13). Those who can see this structural violence have been cowed into silence. Many of the rich and prosperous are living lifestyles which are insensitive to the needs of the poor (6:4-7). The rich tend to see their prosperity (if they think in these terms at all) as evidence of divine approval and favour, and the plight of the poor and those economically disadvantaged as evidence of divine punishment. The problem is the lack of solidarity in society; its cause materialism. Amos wants to see a return to covenant religion: "For thus says the Lord to the house of Israel: seek me and live" (5:4).

> *"I believe in the Holy Spirit, the Lord and giver of life ... who has spoken through the prophets."* Nicene Creed
>
> *In the Judeo-Christian tradition the prophetic literature is regarded as inspired literature. The writings of prophets like Isaiah, Jeremiah, Ezekiel, Amos and Hosea are part of the canon of scripture in the Bible. This incorporation in the canon is a recognition that these writings are not only praiseworthy and instructive; these writings have both divine and human authorship. The Holy Spirit has inspired these preachers/writers with a message of salvation. The Holy Spirit has spoken through these prophets.*

The structure of the Book of Amos

We could divide the canonical *Book of Amos* into three basic parts:

1:3-2:16	oracles against the nations
3:1-6:14	short oracles
7:1-9:15	vision reports

The first section of the *Book*, the oracles against the nations, is a standard feature of prophetic literature and we find similar material in *Jeremiah* (46-51), *Isaiah* (13-19), and *Ezekiel* (25-32). The oracles in Amos work on a 3+4 formula. Amos identifies crimes of terror, crimes against humanity and crimes against the natural law in Israel's neighbours (Damascus, Gaza, Tyre, Edom, Ammon, Moab) before focusing his attack on Israel and Judah. He prophesies against Judah, his home kingdom, for abandoning covenant religion (2:4). He prophesies against Israel, his host kingdom, for blatant crimes of social justice and sexual immorality (2:6-8). This is a people who have lost their collective memory (2:9-11). Punishment is coming in the form of military defeat (2:12-16).

The second section or division of the canonical *Book* is the collection of short oracles (3:1-6:14). Again, Amos sees the present dilemma in terms of a society which has forgotten its story and so has lost its way. Israel must remember and recover its traditions or stories of exodus and election (3:1-2). Recovery of the past and remembrance of the sacred traditions of the past is the only way to the future. Amos preaches on social injustice, excessive lifestyle (4:1-3), a corrupt cult (5:21-27) and lack of solidarity. He sees a direct connection between these socio-economic evils and divine punishment in terms of disasters such as drought (4:7-9) and military defeat (4:10). What is needed is justice and righteousness (5:24). Otherwise divine punishment is going to come on society in terms of the Day of the Lord (5:18-20).

The third section of the *Book* is the five vision reports (7:1-9:15). These reports are oftentimes dramatic and engaging ways of presenting his message. Amos sees visions of locusts (7:1-3), drought (7:4-6), a plumb-line, used for building construction (7:7-9), a basket of fruit (8:1-3), and the dramatic destruction of the sanctuary (9:1-4). These dramatic visions as oracles of judgement offer little hope. At times Amos is successful at interceding with the Lord (7:3, 6); at other times he is reduced to silence at the appalling nature of what he sees. It is easy to see the contemporary relevance of what Amos was preaching. Much of the socio-economic violence he identifies in his own society is still present in contemporary society. Amos basically wanted to rattle society's cage, to challenge complacency, blindness to social evil, to call his contemporaries to reconsider their relationship with the Lord. A society which has forgotten its (religious) past, in his terms, was a society which had little future.

Prophetic language and imagery of Amos

Amos was an inspiring and resourceful preacher. His message is not just simply doom and gloom. He seeks to engage his target audience with the message in ways which will have dramatic effect. He is a consummate salesman. He uses the messenger formula "thus says the Lord" (1:6, 13; 2:1, 6; 3:11, 12; 5:3, 4, 16; 7:17) to great effect, to establish his credentials as prophet and messenger of the Lord. The vision reports (7:1-9; 8:1-3; 9:1-4) are dramatic ways of presenting his message, drawing on experiences such as drought, plague and political instability with which his audience would have been very familiar. He uses graded, numerical sayings, the 3+4 pattern, to structure his message for maximum effect (1:3-2:16). He uses antithesis, contrasting two things together, and especially to demonstrate that expected results of behaviour do not necessarily materialise: do not seek God in religious shrines (where you might expect to encounter the Lord), but rather seek God in justice and righteousness (5:4-7). He also cleverly uses word plays in his prophecy. A good example of this literary technique is to be found in 8:1-2 where Amos sees a basket of summer fruit. In the Hebrew there is a clever word play on "basket of summer fruit" and "the end". He also uses similes, this is like that, drawing on contextual and agricultural imagery his audience would be familiar with and know (6:12). Literary technique, then, is key to the effective presentation of his message.

The message of Amos: religion is no substitute for justice

The central message of Amos' preaching is the call for justice: "let justice roll down like waters, and righteousness like an ever flowing stream"(5:24). He makes this call for justice in the face of what he sees as endemic corruption, systemic evil (5:11-13) and a vulgar, insensitive lifestyle on the part of the rich (6:4-7). A society which does not have justice and solidarity as its base is a society far removed from covenant religion. Piety is no substitute for justice (5:4-7). True religion and justice must go hand in hand. Amos preaches a God who rejects formalised religion and ritual cult which does not also practice justice (5:21-27). The shrines and cultic centres have become breeding grounds for sacrilege. Religion is protecting its power and vested interest (7:10-17) rather than promoting justice and protecting the vulnerable. The weak and the powerless are being exploited, literally sold as commodities in trade (2:6-8). The rich maintain a lifestyle which is grossly insensitive to the needs of the poor, building ivory palaces while many remain homeless, evicted from ancestral lands (3:15). Lip service to religion is common while economic exploitation is rife (8:4-7). With passion and attention to detail Amos offers an unrelenting judgement on the society of Israel, far removed from the Lord because it is far removed from justice and solidarity, even while that same society goes merrily on its way to ruin. The Day of the Lord as the day of judgement is coming (5:18-20).

The vision reports of Amos (7:1-9; 8:1-3)

The five vision reports of Amos are contained in chapters 7-9 of the canonical *Book*. We can

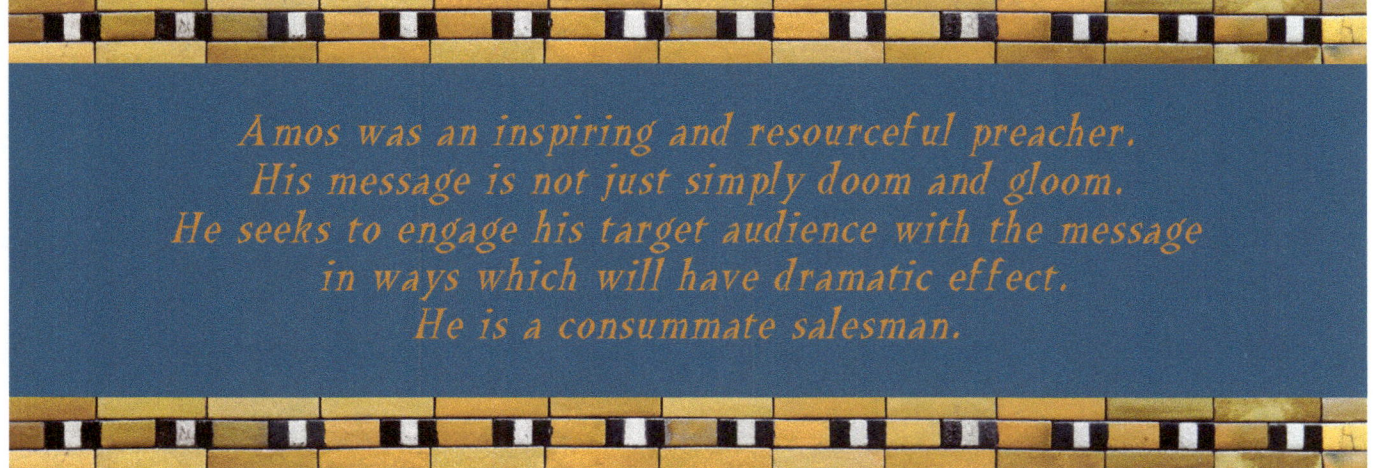

Amos was an inspiring and resourceful preacher. His message is not just simply doom and gloom. He seeks to engage his target audience with the message in ways which will have dramatic effect. He is a consummate salesman.

now look at four of these visions, the locusts (7:1-3), the great fire (7:4-6), the plumb-line (7:7-9), and the basket of summer fruit (8:1-3) as texts which illustrate the message of the prophet as well as his literary skill in imagery and technique. Each of these vision texts begins with the phrase "this is what the Lord God showed me" (7:1, 4, 7; 8:1), indicating a discrete literary unit. The episode of the confrontation between Amos and Amaziah (7:10-17) is placed among the vision reports because of the textual reference to Jeroboam II, king of Israel (7:9, 10). A vision report is a common enough literary form in the prophetic literature. In the *Book of Jeremiah*, for example, we find a similar vision report of an almond tree and a cooking pot (1:11-13), common place objects from daily life which then assume a prophetic even ominous significance when interpreted by the Lord (1:14-19).

The vision reports in Amos follow the same basic structure: a report of what is seen, the prophet's response and the Lord's response. In the first and second visions, the visions of the locusts and the great fire, the Lord responds to the prophet's intercession and nullifies the impending disaster. In the third and fourth visions, the vision of the plumb-line and the basket of summer fruit, Amos does not attempt intercession and the judgement of God in the form of an impending disaster is seen as absolute. The four visions are of different types, even if they have a similar structure: an event (a locust plague), a metaphor (the fire of the great deep), an image (a plumb-line, used for construction), and a clever word play (a basket of summer fruit or the end). The visions are dramatic ways of presenting the message of impending judgement. All four vision reports contain dialogue between Amos and the Lord. The prophet is an active participant in the vision, not just simply in terms of being interlocutor with the Lord, but also in exercising his key prophetic role and function of intercessor. Amos clearly understands his role here as intercessor with the Lord on behalf of the sinful nation, identified as "Jacob" (7:2, 5). We note there is no commission from the Lord to Amos to reveal or preach these vision reports to the community. Amos ceases to intercede for Israel after the second vision report. We examine now each of these four vision reports in turn.

The first vision (7:1-3) is a locust swarm

In an agricultural society such a natural disaster is a particularly grave threat. We see this image used in other prophetic books as a symbol of approaching disaster (*Joel* 1:4). The locusts appear at a particularly vulnerable time in the cycle of harvests, after the harvests for the

The change of heart on the Lord's part, we might say, indicates the action of one who has been deeply moved. Amos has appealed to the tradition of a gracious and merciful God.

This is an intense image of total destruction, the obliteration of the world as they envisaged it.

royal stables, a king's prerogative. The community faces the spectre of famine. The locusts devour all the vegetation. Amos pleads and intercedes with the Lord to avert such a disaster. The guilty (described here as "Jacob") are presented as helpless before such a threat. The Lord relents. Amos has been successful in his intercession, as Moses had been successful in his intercession with the Lord (*Exodus* 34:6-7). There is no indication in this vision report, however, of divine pardon, simply the removal of this natural disaster. What Amos has done in this vision report is to give an account of what he has seen, offered an interpretation, and then pleaded with the Lord to avert such a disaster. The change of heart on the Lord's part, we might say, indicates the action of one who has been deeply moved. Amos has appealed to the tradition of a gracious and merciful God.

The second vision report (7:4-6) is of a devouring fire

Unlike the first vision which deals with a disaster in nature, this vision is more of the nature of a metaphor, a huge, destructive fire (more than a bushfire!) which consumes the world and the great deep of water. The image of the "great deep" is a stylistic way of referring to the cosmos as the Hebrew people understood the world, its foundations on the waters, and the heavens (*Genesis* 7:11; *Isaiah* 51:10). This is an intense image of total destruction, the obliteration of the world as they envisaged it. In the imagination of Amos' audience the experience of prolonged drought (a not unusual occurrence) could portend the force of such a metaphoric disaster. Again, we see Amos appalled at what the vision suggests and the helplessness of the guilty "Jacob" before such a form of divine punishment. Amos intercedes again successfully with the Lord and we see the same pattern in this second vision report as in the first report: the Lord relents. Again we see that the punishment is annulled but there is no necessary indication of divine forgiveness. Amos is a second Moses, pleading for his guilty people (*Exodus* 32:10-14).

The third vision report (7:7-9) concerns a plumb line

We are dealing now not with a natural disaster or a catastrophe but a material object, possibly used on a building site. A plumb line, held in the builder's hand, is used to measure accuracy, to ensure the wall is even and will not collapse. We have a particular problem in interpreting and reading this vision report as the Hebrew word used here for

what the NRSV translates as "plumb line" is a *hapaxlegomenon*, that is, a word which occurs only once in the Hebrew scriptures (used four times here in this vision report) and so we can only ascertain its meaning from the context and from similar words and contexts (*Isaiah* 28:17). The Lord holds a material object in his hand which Amos clearly sees and which he clearly identifies. There is a pattern here of question and response, which has not been in the first two vision reports. While Amos clearly identifies the object held by the Lord, he needs to be instructed, however, on its metaphoric meaning, that is, the object portends and signifies approaching judgement. We note how a plain, simple object, held in the hand, can assume such significance, portending disaster. The context suggests it is an object of judgement. This judgement will assume two forms: destruction of high places and sanctuaries associated with worship and punishment of the house of Jeroboam (king in the northern kingdom of Israel, with Samaria as capital city). The plumb line suggests that the wall (symbol of the northern kingdom) is poised perilously and is about to collapse in ruins. Amos does not attempt intercession.

The fourth vision report (8:1-3) concerns a basket of summer fruit or first fruit from the harvest

Again we have a similar issue of interpretation here as with the third vision. While the Hebrew word is clear enough suggesting a basket of summer fruit, there is also a clever play on words here between the word for "summer fruit" (*qayits*) and a similar sounding word meaning "the end" (*qets*) or reaping time. Thus Amos has skilfully used alliteration and play on words in the hearing of his target audience (or was it his southern accent?) to suggest two related but different meanings: a word meaning the enjoyment of summer harvest and a similar word suggesting not enjoyment but approaching judgement. While the third vision report relied on the symbolic value of a material object (a plumb line) for its impact, this fourth vision relies on a word play. Again we see the same pattern in this report as in the previous report: vision, question, response, interpretation. We are reminded of a similar vision and similar structure in Jeremiah's vision of the almond tree (*Jeremiah* 1:11-12). Amos again identifies the object (basket of summer fruit) without hesitation. Again, Amos does not attempt intercession. This fourth vision report is presented as the climactic announcement of judgement: "the end has come upon my people Israel". The Lord can no longer simply ignore the apostasy of his people. Songs shall become lamentations and dirges. There will be many corpses. As if violent death were not enough punishment, the vision also announces further degradation and humiliation in the form of unburied bodies. In the Old Testament such a fate was the ultimate shame (*Jeremiah* 16:4). The fourth vision report announces the end which has been ominously suggested in the first three vision reports.

Amos, a skilful practitioner

The four vision reports firstly reveal the great literary skill and insight of Amos in presenting his prophetic message from the Lord to his target audience in the northern kingdom. His use of imagery (first, second and third visions), alliteration and word play (fourth vision) demonstrate his skill and ability in making a dramatic impact on his audience in such a way that they will hear, receive and remember his message. Secondly, the vision reports give us a sustained insight and understanding into one of the key functions of the Hebrew prophet, that of intercession. Amos pleads successfully with the Lord for mercy for the guilty in the first two vision reports. In this function he appears to be performing the same ministry as Moses did. Amos is able to intercede with the Lord because the God of Israel is also the God of compassion. The God of the prophets is a God who is holy, merciful and just. Amos as intercessor appeals to this tradition of the God of forbearance. If you will, Amos is learning the skill and trade

> *Thus Amos has skilfully used alliteration and play on words in the hearing of his target audience (or was it his southern accent?) to suggest two related but different meanings: a word meaning the enjoyment of summer harvest and a similar word suggesting not enjoyment but approaching judgement.*

of prophetic intercession in these visions. God reveals the divine plans to his servants the prophets (3:7). These are privileged persons interceding for the guilty. And yet the four vision reports are not all doom and gloom. Hidden away, almost imperceptibly in two of the vision reports, is the simple but affectionate appellation the Lord uses for the target audience, the phrase "my people" (7:8; 8:2). Guilty and under judgement this is a people still precious to the Lord. As with Moses, so now with Amos, there is a fine balance to be struck between punishment on the one hand and mercy on the other. This key movement and divine sentiment is expressed beautifully in *Hosea* 11:1-11.

SUMMARY

- Amos was an eighth century prophet called to ministry in the northern kingdom of Israel.
- The times were relatively peaceful and secure with economic prosperity. Amos preached that this wealth was based on exploitation of an underclass.
- Amos prophesied the fall of the northern kingdom which came to pass in 722 BCE.
- The text 7:10-17, the confrontation with the priest Amaziah, gives us a snapshot of Amos' life and his calling as a prophet.
- He had the gift of a true insight into the nature of his society: it lacked justice.
- Good people were demoralised by what they saw around them (systemic corruption) but were cowed into silence.
- The vision reports (7:1-9; 8:1-3) give us a good understanding of Amos' message and his skill as a speaker.

CHAPTER THREE

Hosea

THE ENDURING LOVE OF GOD

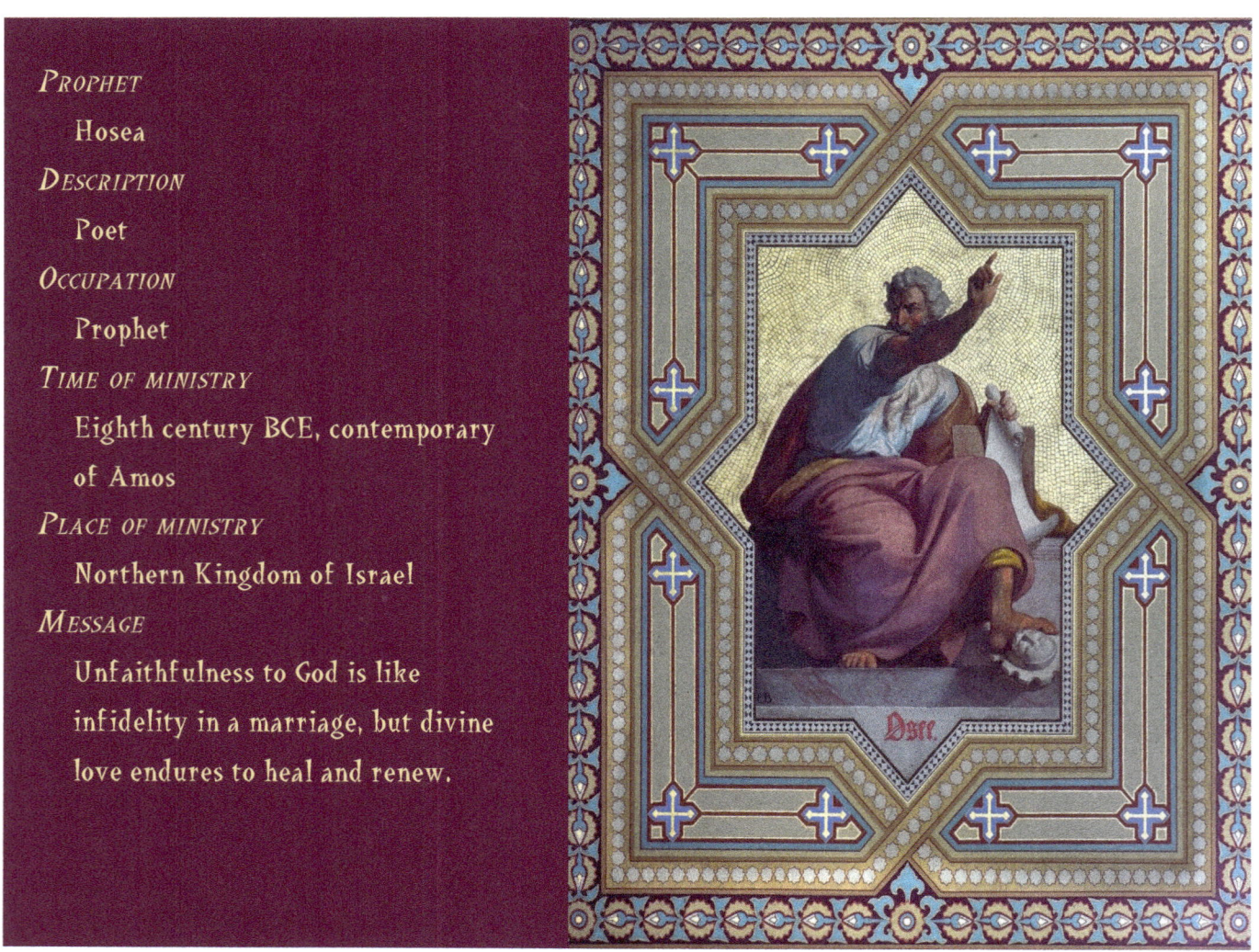

PROPHET
  Hosea
DESCRIPTION
  Poet
OCCUPATION
  Prophet
TIME OF MINISTRY
  Eighth century BCE, contemporary of Amos
PLACE OF MINISTRY
  Northern Kingdom of Israel
MESSAGE
  Unfaithfulness to God is like infidelity in a marriage, but divine love endures to heal and renew.

> *I led them with cords of human kindness, with bands of love. I bent down to them and fed them.*
> Hosea 11:4

The prophet Hosea and the religious context of his preaching in Israel

Hosea was a younger contemporary of the prophet Amos. Apart from the superscription of his prophecy (1:1) which identifies the kings of Israel and Judah at the time of his ministry, we know few personal details about the prophet. The references to these kings would place his ministry around the years 750-724 BCE. Hosea was a northern prophet, from the kingdom of Israel. There is no mention in his prophecy of the catastrophic events of 722 BCE and the disappearance of the kingdom of Israel as a state and its absorption as provinces into the Assyrian empire. Nevertheless, there are many references in his prophecy to the turbulent and violent history of the northern kingdom which Hosea witnessed. Hosea was obsessed by the worship of the Baals in Israel and the nation's apostate religious practices. We might identify these religious practices as syncretism, that is, the absorption of pagan religious cultic practices into monotheistic religion (the worship of the Lord) with the result that the strength and identity of Israel's religion became increasingly diluted and weak, however popular such practices may have been to a population who saw such religious relativism as inoffensive and indeed consistent with religious practice in other nations of the region. Hosea was a trenchant opponent of this syncretism and specifically of the Baals. He saw his society as rushing headlong to self-inflicted destruction: "thus a people without understanding comes to ruin" (4:14). Forgetfulness of God leads to loss of national identity. As well, being a small, petty state in the world of the Ancient Near East, surrounded by the superpower Assyria, Israel had to make many political compromises in order to simply survive. For Hosea such alliances placed the religious values of his country under significant pressure.

The structure of the Book of Hosea

The canonical *Book of Hosea*, as we have it in the Bible, could be read in two parts: chapters 1-3 concern the marriage metaphor Hosea uses so effectively in his preaching, and chapters 4-14 are a collection of prophetic oracles addressed to the northern kingdom. There is some evidence in the *Book* of redaction and editing of his prophetic oracles by scribes in the southern kingdom of Judah, sometime after Hosea, to present his preaching as relevant also for their situation (1:7;3:5;11:12;14:9). The *Book* evidences significant literary sophistication and style. We can briefly look at its twofold structure.

Marriage metaphor

Hosea's language about God in chapters 1-4 is highly metaphoric and symbolic, particularly the image of God as the aggrieved husband of a faithless wife. The unfaithful wife and indeed the

---

"It is the quality and profundity of the prophetic utterance, its piercing theistic vision, its exceptional moral discernment and the anguish with which it is touched (for prophets do not arrive at the truth without suffering for it), which make it a word of God. The canonical prophets were not spell-binders or practitioners of sympathetic magic." William McKane

This quotation identifies one of the key features of being a prophet in ancient Israel: the human and personal cost. An encounter with the word of the living God was a searing experience (Ezekiel 8:1; Daniel 8:27). A prophet could not preach with disinterest. There was always the personal cost and the personal anguish involved. Jeremiah described this experience as like a fire in his bones, God like a deceitful brook, and yet the word a joy and delight to him (15:15-18). The prophets were not God's messenger boys. Being a messenger of the Lord required great personal understanding and appropriation of that word before giving the word to others. Prophets were not interested in being popular, giving people what they wanted to hear. The ministry of the prophet was to afflict the comfortable, and comfort the afflicted (Amos 6:4-7).

erring woman is a consistent enough image used by the prophets to depict a nation's apostasy from its God (see *Ezekiel* 16:1-63). The negativity of this image needs to be kept in mind when reading and interpreting such passages. Chapters 1-3 present a shocking, confronting image of Hosea being called by the Lord to marry a prostitute (Gomer) or a woman with a reputation for promiscuous behaviour (1:2). The children of this union are to bear highly symbolic names: "Jezreel" (with reference to the violent Jehu dynasty), "not pitied" and "not my people" (1:4-8). The marriage and the children act out in a highly symbolic fashion — almost as a pantomime — the relationship between Israel and the Lord. It is a moot point whether Hosea actually had intercourse with Gomer (see 3:3) but the confronting nature of the union proposed communicated the divine intent of infidelity on Israel's part to the Lord in an effective manner. This image of marital infidelity is also used in chapter 2 in the context of the legal proceeding the Lord brings against Israel in the courts. Divorce proceedings and punishment of the unfaithful wife in the court forms the dramatic background to this image Hosea uses.

Adultery as metaphor

The adultery Hosea so graphically depicts is not in fact sexual relations with another man but a striking image or symbol of the worship of the Baals in Israel. This was a Canaanite religious system or practice involving rites of fertility. In an arid, dry land the continuation of the cycles of nature, and particularly of rain, was seen as ensured through participation in these cultic practices. For Hosea true fertility comes from the Lord (2:8) and not from such pagan practices. The wilderness tradition when Israel was led through the Sinai desert for 40 years under the leadership of Moses was an especially important and appealing tradition for Hosea. This was the time when Israel was at its best and most faithful (a rather idealising reading we might say) and so the Lord wishes to draw Israel back to the wilderness time and experience as the way of recovering lost fidelity: "therefore, I will now allure her, and bring her into the wilderness, and speak tenderly to her" (2:14). What Hosea wishes to depict, then, is the hope for a new beginning. The Exodus and the wilderness tradition become the paradigm of the new beginning. Whatever the elegance or historical accuracy of the metaphor of the unfaithful wife being lured into the wilderness — all metaphors limp to some degree and we need to pay particular attention to the negative stereotyping of women here — Hosea is making a very real point about Israel's religious tradition and history: a nation which has forgotten its past has no future (4:14). The image Hosea uses of the Lord as the aggrieved husband and Israel as the unfaithful wife is an image or metaphor about power in relationships. We note also the appropriateness here of Gomer as the adulterous wife rather than the prostitute, as adultery carries the connotations of infidelity and not just simply promiscuity (1:2).

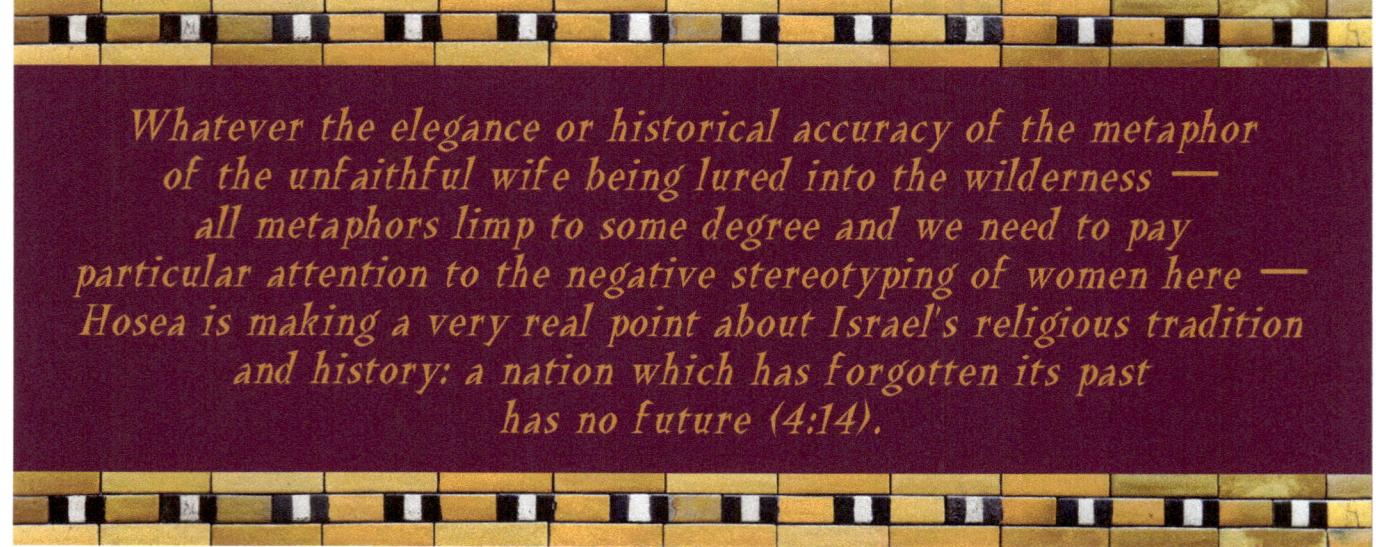

Whatever the elegance or historical accuracy of the metaphor of the unfaithful wife being lured into the wilderness — all metaphors limp to some degree and we need to pay particular attention to the negative stereotyping of women here — Hosea is making a very real point about Israel's religious tradition and history: a nation which has forgotten its past has no future (4:14).

Oracles of judgement and salvation

The second division in the structure of the *Book of Hosea* is chapters 4-14 which contain the oracles the prophet delivered to his target audience in Israel. This second division of the *Book* in fact falls into two parts: a collection of oracles of judgement in chapters 4-11 and a collection of oracles of salvation in chapters 12-14, a typical enough structure of a prophetic book. Hosea indicts his audience of sins and crimes against the Decalogue (4:1-2). For him covenant and law are directly linked (8:1). Hosea's view of the world and the society of his time is a simple one, but not a simplistic one: Israel's world is based on covenant fidelity and when this is ruptured or compromised, chaos ensues (4:3). Images of fertility in nature and marital fidelity are simply graphic and imaginative ways of presenting this central insight. Fidelity to God is an enduring prophetic concern. There is evidence in the *Book of Hosea* of his oracles being redacted and edited long after his death in order to present the relevance and pertinence of his teaching to subsequent generations (3:5; 11:12).

What is it the Lord really wants?

For Hosea what the Lord really requires, what God is really looking for is righteousness, steadfast love and knowledge of God. These are the staples of covenant religion. In two of the oracles the Lord speaks about what is required: "for I desire steadfast love and not sacrifice, the knowledge of God rather than burnt offerings" (6:6), and again, "sow for yourselves righteousness; reap steadfast love; break up your fallow ground; for it is time to seek the Lord, that he may come and rain righteousness upon you." (10:12). There is nothing new in this message from the Lord through the prophet Hosea to the people of Israel. The key aspects of covenant religion which the Lord wants— righteousness, steadfast love, knowledge of God — were well known to the audience but simply now forgotten or compromised. Forgetfulness of past, then, is one of the key issues Hosea identifies. This people has forgotten or lost its story of covenant love and fidelity with the Lord, what we might call its metanarrative. Consequently, it has no future: "thus a people without understanding comes to ruin" (4:14). The other concern of Hosea, the other part of his devastating critique, is the way in which religion and cult have led people astray. Religion is understood as simply lip-service to God in cult (4:7-19). Religion is taking people away from the Lord rather than closer to their God. Forgetfulness of foundation story and key beliefs and reliance on religion as a mechanical means of relating to God has led Israel dangerously away from what God really wants. We notice how skilfully Hosea appeals to memory and history (metanarrative) as the way to the future. Such an authoritative reading and such an authoritative text would be taken up by subsequent generations of scribes and prophets as a way of interpreting the religious climate of their own time.

Images of fertility in nature and marital fidelity are simply graphic and imaginative ways of presenting this central insight. Fidelity to God is an enduring prophetic concern.

The poetic language and imagery of Hosea

Hosea is a highly descriptive, highly imaginative prophet and poet. He uses set prophetic oracular forms, like the legal dispute form, as well as original imagery to present the Lord and Israel in his message and, as we have seen with the Gomer stories, symbolic actions. One of the set prophetic oracular forms Hosea uses is the legal dispute form from the courts, what is known as the *rib* form in Hebrew. This is cast in the form of a legal indictment. Hosea uses this form at least twice in his message (4:1; 12:2). God is presented as plaintiff and judge, Israel is presented as defendant. While the outcome is thus assured, the purpose of the process is to clearly identify Israel's failures in covenant, specifically in terms of the decalogue (ten commandments). The key elements of covenant fidelity are missing (4:1) and instead there is a catalogue of crimes (4:2). Hosea borrows from the legal dispute form, familiar to his hearers. Such a process took place at the city gates to ensure the trial was open and transparent. Hosea's intention is using this form was to indict his own people of cultic idolatry with the hope of bringing about a change of heart. People lack understanding (4:14) because they lack knowledge (4:6), and they lack knowledge because they have not been properly instructed (4:4-6). The priests are the particular target for this ignorance in Hosea's legal dispute form (4:6-13). The *rib* form is a highly imaginative literary form the prophet uses to clarify what exactly is the issue and what exactly it is that the Lord requires.

Hosea's prophecy is also full of the most extraordinary images about the Lord and about Israel. He graphically describes both in ways which are quite striking and original. The Lord is described as being like a husband (1:2-3:5), a cypress tree (14:8), an enraged she-bear robbed of her cubs (13:8), a parent (11:1-11), a lion and a leopard (5:14; 13:7), and finally, most striking of all images, like gangrene and maggots (5:12). Israel is described as being like a wife (2:19), a flighty dove (7:11), a grapevine (9:10), morning dew (6:4), a sick person (5:13), a stubborn heifer (4:16), a heated oven (7:4), smoke (13:3), and like burnt cake (7:8). All of these images are familiar to Hosea's audience from everyday life. Hosea uses them in ways which are striking, evocative, imaginative. As we have also seen, Hosea uses symbolic action to great effect with the marriage to Gomer and the names given to the children. Hosea is not only a prophet of the Lord, but a skilful poet in the delivery of this message.

SUMMARY

- Hosea was an eighth century prophet in Israel, like his contemporary Amos.
- He saw Israel as a nation rushing to ruin, forgetful of its God.
- His prophecy displays great literary sophistication, especially in chapters 1-3 on the marriage metaphor.
- Hosea was convinced that forgetfulness of the traditions of the past means that a nation has no future.
- Fidelity to God was an enduring concern.
- Hosea taught that what God really wants is righteousness, steadfast love and knowledge of God.
- Hosea was a great poet as well as prophet, using a wealth of images and ideas to communicate his message.
- 11:1-11 is one of the classic texts in the Old Testament about the patience and endurance of divine love.

Hosea 11:1-11 a classic text of God's parental and nurturing love for Israel

One of the classic texts of divine love in the Old Testament is this beautiful oracle in Hosea about God's love for Israel being like that of a parent nurturing a young child or infant. It would be hard to find a more striking image of divine love. God's love is presented in terms of tender attentiveness to the child and refusal to abandon the child even when that love is unrequited. The oracle balances the love of God on the one hand and the obstinacy of the child Israel on the other. It is again presented from the point of view of the metanarrative, recalling the great events of the past, in the form of an intense historical retrospect. The Hebrew verb *shuv* "to return", used as a staple term for conversion in the prophetic literature, is used in two senses in the oracle: a return to the Lord and a turning away from the Lord (verse 7). Israel as the obstinate child is referred to in the third person in verses 1-7 but then directly addressed in verses 8-9. Divine love is unwavering: always ready to excuse, to trust, to hope for return. It is this divine love which makes possible the salvation now approaching (verses 10-11) even in the face of Israel's obstinate or (at best) changing love and allegiance. The historical retrospect is presented in terms of the Exodus story tradition so favoured by Hosea: the journey from Egypt and the seemingly necessary return to Egypt. Let us briefly look at this oracle verse by verse.

Verse one: The oracle begins in the Exodus tradition from slavery in Egypt, the beginnings of the salvation story. Two words are used to describe Israel: "child" and "son". This person is an infant, a very young person, even a toddler perhaps. The child is totally dependent on the adult for sustenance, care, affection. The father figure provides care, protection, guidance, providence. It is a beautiful image of human intimacy between father and son as a metaphor for divine love.

Verse two: The problem issue now becomes apparent within the historical retrospect. The Hebrew verb for "call" is also the verb for metaphoric choice of Israel by God. But as God calls, Israel turns away. The movement of turning away becomes a metaphor for apostasy. Apostasy here is the cult of the Baals. In the wilderness wandering too there was the repeated desire to return to the safety of Egypt.

Verse three: We note the contrast between "I" and "they", between the divine actions of election and love and Israel's actions of obstinate refusal. It is almost as if God sees this action as incomprehensible. God has been the nurturing parent, guiding the first, hesitant steps of the young infant.

Verse four: The image of the nurturing parent is more fully developed with great tenderness and warmth. As a loving parent instinctively holds the infant child to his/her cheek to convey in the softness of warm flesh against warm flesh the tenderness of love, so God regarded Israel. As a parent stoops down to meet the infant in his/her little world to give sustenance and provide what is needed, beyond the capacities of the little child to provide for itself, so God fed Israel.

Verse five: Our key verb *shuv* "to return" now appears in the oracle in the two fold sense of returning in punishment to the land of Egypt (and so frustrating the cycle of exodus from Egypt in the first place) because they have not returned (in repentance) to the Lord.

Verse six: This was a society very familiar with the violence of warfare and the destruction of foreign invasion and incursion. One can almost sense the enraged swishing of the sword! The northern kingdom was under constant threat from its military superpower Assyria to the north.

Verse seven: The Lord speaks in passionate terms: "my people" turning away "from me". Despite the obstinacy and the unrequited love the Lord calls Israel "my people". This apostasy is unfathomable.

Verse eight: God's heart is, as it were, torn between undying affection and love for Israel and the need for punishment for its apostasy. The theme of divine remorse and compassion is a familiar one in the prophetic literature (*Isaiah* 57:18; *Zechariah* 1:13) but this laying bare, as it were, of God's inner struggle is unsurpassed. The Lord cannot abandon Israel. The reference to Admah and Zeboiim recalls the fate of Sodom and

Gomorrah (*Deuteronomy* 29:23): the destruction of all life and the possibility of new life. God cannot abandon Israel to this fate. Divine anger now gives way to divine compassion.

Verse nine: We note the use of the word "not" three times in this verse, indicating decisive, considered behaviour. Divine action is not like the way human beings act. The Lord is, as it were, in control of the divine emotions. God will not act in anger and God will not punish. We note also that God refers to the divine self as "the Holy One", a title for God preferred by the prophet Isaiah.

Verse ten: Hosea introduces a new image of God now, that of a lion, and a lion roaring! We have seen this image earlier (5:14). We have moved from a parental image to one now of nature. Israel is still referred to as "his children". The reference to the west could be one about the exile.

Verse eleven: The references to Egypt and Assyria are references to lands of exile and oppression. The nature image of verse ten of the Lord as a lion is complemented here now with the image of Israel as a dove, but not the flighty dove we have seen (7:11) but almost as a homing pigeon, purposefully and instinctively returning to its nest. Israel is coming home! Again we see Hosea skilfully using the key Hebrew verb *shuv,* indicating it is God who will bring them home. This homecoming is the divine initiative. It is divine love which makes this return possible.

HOSEA 11: 1-11

1 When Israel was a child, I loved him,
and out of Egypt I called my son.
2 The more I called them, the more they went from me;
they kept sacrificing to the Baals, and offering incense to idols.
3 Yet it was I who taught Ephraim to walk,
I took them up in my arms;
but they did not know that I healed them.
4 I led them with cords of human kindness, with bands of love.
I was to them like those who lift infants to their cheeks.
I bent down to them and fed them.

5 They shall return to the land of Egypt,
and Assyria shall be their king,
because they have refused to return to me.
6 The sword rages in their cities,
it consumes their oracle priests,
and devours because of their schemes.
7 My people are bent on turning away from me.
To the Most High they call,
but he does not raise them up at all.

8 How can I give you up, Ephraim?
How can I hand you over, O Israel?
How can I make you like Admah?
How can I treat you like Zeboiim?
My heart recoils within me;
 my compassion grows warm and tender.
9 I will not execute my fierce anger;
I will not again destroy Ephraim;
for I am God and no mortal,
the Holy One in your midst, and I will not come in wrath.

10 They shall go after the Lord, who roars like a lion;
when he roars, his children shall come trembling from the west.
11 They shall come trembling like birds from Egypt,
and like doves from the land of Assyria;
and I will return them to their homes, says the Lord.

CHAPTER FOUR

Jeremiah

RELUCTANT PROPHET

Prophet
  Jeremiah
Description
  Reluctant Prophet
Occupation
  Priest
Time of ministry
  Sixth century BCE
Place of ministry
  Kingdom of Judah and city of Jerusalem
Message
  God promises a new covenant in the face of the political, social and religious collapse of Judah.

❝ *The days are surely coming, says the Lord, when I will make a new covenant with the house of Israel and the house of Judah.* ❞

Jeremiah 31:31

The prophet Jeremiah and the religious and political context of his preaching

By the time the prophet Jeremiah began his preaching ministry, the kingdom of Judah with its capital Jerusalem had been reduced to a rump state from the great empire of David and Solomon. The northern kingdom of Israel had been incorporated into the Assyrian empire a century before Jeremiah began preaching in Jerusalem. Judah was a small, petty state of no great military significance except for its strategic significance in the struggles between the great superpowers of the Ancient Near East. The dates of Jeremiah's life and prophetic ministry are generally given as 627 BCE until sometime after 587 BCE. He lived through several of the great watershed events of his time in terms of their political significance for the kingdom of Judah.

In 609 BCE Josiah, king of Judah, was killed in battle at Megiddo, attempting to halt an Egyptian army passing through his territory to assist the Assyrians against the Babylonians. This was a traumatic loss of a great reforming king. In 605 BCE the Babylonians under Nebuchadnezzar annihilated the same Egyptian army at Carchemish. The strategic balance of the Ancient Near East was changed dramatically and almost overnight with the Babylonians now in the ascent as the major superpower. Small states like Judah were forced to realign their strategic interests in order to survive. Babylon was to cast a long shadow. Finally, Jeremiah lived through the two Babylonian sieges of Jerusalem in 597 BCE and 587 BCE, witnessing at first hand in the final siege the complete destruction of the city and state. To say that Jeremiah lived in interesting times would be something of an understatement!

Jeremiah as another Moses

The dates given for Jeremiah's life and prophetic ministry (627 BCE – sometime after 587 BCE) are highly symbolic themselves. It is a matter of conjecture among scholars whether the date 627 BCE represents the date of his prophetic call by the Lord (1:4-19) or the date of his birth, called to be a prophet from his mother's womb. After the capture and destruction of Jerusalem by the Babylonians following the second siege, Jeremiah was taken, against his will, into Egypt with the other refugees (43:6-7). He continued his prophetic ministry there (44-45) and presumably died in Egypt. The dates given for Jeremiah amount to forty years, corresponding to the forty years in the wilderness. Jeremiah is also presented as a prophet like Moses. The reader is invited to see a symbolic association between Moses and Jeremiah: Moses led the tribes out of Egypt; Jeremiah is forced to return to Egypt. Prophecy has gone full circle.

Deuteronomic reform

Mention has been made here of King Josiah. As ruler of Judah Josiah had actively supported and promoted what has become known as the Deuteronomic reform, the purpose of which was to reform the cult and practise of religion in Judah according to the teaching of the *Book of Deuteronomy*. While we can assume Jeremiah would have been largely sympathetic to the general thrust of these reforms, curiously he says very little about the reform in his preaching. He does compare Josiah's son and successor Jehoiakim unfavourably with his father, particularly in matters of social justice (22:13-19), but the reform itself does not figure prominently. Josiah had attempted a number of measures to revitalise faith according to the principles of *Deuteronomy*,

> "The prophet is one who has combined an extraordinary religious impressionability with a fineness of moral fibre."
> Abraham Kuenen, quoted by William McKane

The prophet was a person who was in a profound personal relationship with the Lord (Jeremiah 17:14-18). Being a prophet was not simply a task or a ministry to perform but a calling to enter into a special relationship with the Lord, on behalf of God's people whose intercessor he became. The prophet had first of all to become an intense listener of the word of God himself before he could become a proclaimer of that word to others. What was required of him was an openness, an impressionability to the divine, combined with his own religious and personal moral integrity.

particularly the centralisation of the cult on the Jerusalem temple and the closure of shrines outside the capital city as well as purging the cult of syncretistic and pagan elements. It would seem that with Josiah's death these soon returned and one may ask how effective these reform measures had been, apart from superficial change. Cult and faith were in poor condition when Jeremiah began his prophetic ministry. The threat of Babylon over Judah remained ominous after Carchemish and the first siege of Jerusalem. Jeremiah was present in Jerusalem during the second siege of the city (January 588 BCE – July 587 BCE) and attempted to negotiate, unsuccessfully, the surrender of the city to the Babylonians by the then King Zedekiah (one of Josiah's sons). Interestingly, this meeting was the last encounter in the Old Testament between a king and a prophet (37:1-38:28). Jeremiah witnessed at first hand the traumatic destruction of city, temple, monarchy and state (38:28).

Inner life of Jeremiah

The *Book of Jeremiah* is not only important for what it tells us about the political and religious climate in Judah in the sixth century but also for what it tells us about the inner life of the prophet Jeremiah himself. No other prophetic book gives us such a sustained and penetrating insight and understanding into the inner life of a prophet and what it means, personally and spiritually, for a person to be called by the Lord to the ministry of prophecy and the personal hardship such a calling entails. We are presented with a range of emotions and experiences. These feelings are recorded in the so-called *Lamentations* or *Confessions* of Jeremiah (11:18-12:6; 15:10-21; 17:14-18; 18:18-23; 20:7-18). An anguished heart cries out to the Lord in fear, despair, turmoil. Jeremiah does not mince his words with the Lord: "truly, you are to me like a deceitful brook, like waters that fail" (15:18). His lamentations pour out to the Lord his feelings of isolation and persecution by his neighbours, the personal sense of the failure and futility of his mission, the dryness of his prayer, the intense personal scrutiny he places himself under. Jeremiah is indeed an anguished soul. And yet while these confessions reveal great personal suffering and self-doubt, these same prayers also reveal the depth of the man's relationship with the Lord and the Lord's steadfastness in supporting him (15:19-21).

Jeremiah's life and ministry as witness of his troubled times

One of the great commentators and scholars of the *Book of Jeremiah* is William Holladay who basically approaches the *Book* as a chronological record of the ministry of Jeremiah, that is, the *Book* represents in substantial form the life of the prophet. This view is certainly contested by other scholars. Holladay argues that key speeches of Jeremiah (for example, the famous Temple sermon in 7:1-15; 26:1-14) and key actions (for example, the smashing of the earthenware flask in 19:1-15) can be identified at key moments in Jeremiah's career. Whatever of the theory, Holladay's approach is quite useful in linking the life and ministry of Jeremiah with his troubled and uncertain times. We can reproduce here now in modified form Holladay's reconstruction of the ministry and life of Jeremiah as a witness to a turbulent time in Judah's history:

640 Josiah becomes king of Judah. The nation is a vassal of Assyria whose empire is beginning to fragment.

627 Jeremiah is born in Anathoth, a village north of Jerusalem, of a priestly family.

622 Josiah supports the Deuteronomic reform (*2 Kings* 22-23) with its religious and nationalistic aims.

615 608, 601, 594, 587 septennial reading of the *Book of Deuteronomy* (*Deuteronomy* 31:9-13). This reading process is initiated with the 622 reform. Readings become the context for Jeremiah's preaching as counter-proclamations.

609 Josiah killed at Megiddo. Babylon is a rising world power. Judah is a vassal of Egypt. Jeremiah preaches the Temple sermon.

605 Battle of Carchemish. Nebuchadnezzar's victory over the Egyptians signals a major power shift. Judah becomes a vassal of Babylon. Smashing of the earthenware flask.

597 First Babylonian siege of Jerusalem. Exile of king and nobility to Babylon (including the young priest Ezekiel). Jeremiah writes a letter to the exiles in Babylon (29:1-23) urging them to settle peacefully and maintain hope in the Lord's plans for them.

587 Second Babylonian siege of Jerusalem. Interview between Zedekiah and Jeremiah (37-38). Jeremiah proclaims the new covenant text (31:31-34). Jeremiah in exile in Egypt.

Adapted from William L. Holladay, *Jeremiah 2: A Commentary on the Book of the Prophet Jeremiah Chapters 26-52,* Minneapolis: Fortress Press, 1989, 24-35.

The structure of the Book of Jeremiah

The *Book of Jeremiah* presents significant issues of interpretation to the reader in terms of its structure and the history of its transmission. There are, for example, two versions of the *Book of Jeremiah,* one the Hebrew or Masoretic text (known as MT) and the other the Greek text or Septuagint version (known as LXX). These two versions differ in terms of length (the Hebrew version being longer than the Greek version) and also in the ordering of the materials in the books. As well, there is a variety of prophetic literary forms present in the *Book of Jeremiah*: oracles, prose sermons, biographical narrative and oracles against the nations. There is also specialised material in the *Book,* for example, the book of consolation in chapters 30-33. We could speak then of a number of books or collections within the *Book of Jeremiah*, and this phenomenon itself has generated a number of theories about how the *Book* was edited and redacted over a long period of time into the version(s) we now have. One of the most celebrated of these theories is that of the English scholar William McKane who spoke of a "rolling corpus".

For our purposes here as a general introduction to the *Book* we could identify the following structure:

> *chapters 1-25*
> *   oracles and prose speeches*
> *chapters 26-45*
> *   biographical narrative*
> *   about the prophet Jeremiah*
> *chapters 46-51*
> *   oracles against the nations*
> *chapter 52*
> *   appendix on the fall of*
> *   Jerusalem*

Within chapters 1-25 we find oracles of the prophet and particularly in 2:1-6:30 where we could identify oracles around the themes of the indictment of Judah for its unfaithfulness (2:1-37), the great call for a return to the Lord (3:1-4:4), and the approaching judgement in the form of the "foe from the north" (4:5-6:30). Jeremiah is not dispassionate in his preaching: he feels keenly his own physical, psychological and emotional pain at the forthcoming judgement on his people (4:19-21). The biographical narrative about the prophet (chapters 26-45) could, in fact, be divided into two sections: chapters 26-35 and chapters 36-45. This material may well be the edited work of Jeremiah's companion and scribe Baruch (36:32). The materials appear to be in some chronological order. Interestingly, in the second section (chapters 36-45) there are two occasions where Jeremiah is requested to perform the great prophetic task or function of intercession with the Lord (37:3; 42:2) and so we might speak of two panels within this narrative story. Also within chapters 26-45 we find edited into this material the *Book of Consolation* (chapters 30-33) as specialist material, on a somewhat different theme. In the *Book of Consolation* we find the famous new covenant text (31:31-34). In chapters 46-51 we find the oracles

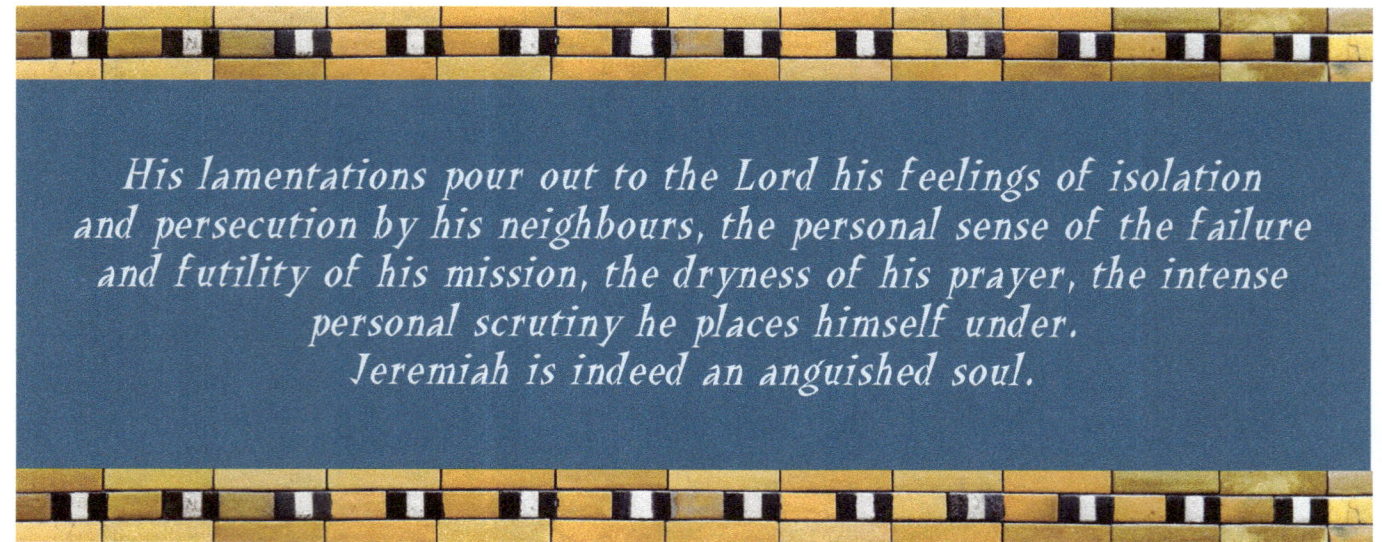

His lamentations pour out to the Lord his feelings of isolation and persecution by his neighbours, the personal sense of the failure and futility of his mission, the dryness of his prayer, the intense personal scrutiny he places himself under.
Jeremiah is indeed an anguished soul.

against the nations, a standard feature of a prophetic book (see *Ezekiel* 25-32; *Isaiah* 13-23; *Amos* 1-2), and especially here the oracle against Babylon (50:1-51:64) the great real and metaphoric enemy of Jeremiah's people. The last chapter of the *Book of Jeremiah* is basically repetition of material from *2 Kings* 24:18-25:30. How and why was this material appended to the *Book of Jeremiah*?

A celebrated Jeremiah text 31:31-34: the new covenant

The most quoted text from the Old Testament in the New is Psalm 110. The second most quoted text is *Jeremiah* 31:31-34, the celebrated announcement of the new covenant. The author of the *Letter to the Hebrews* quotes this text extensively (8:6-13) in his presentation of Jesus as the priest and mediator of a new and greater covenant. Jesus himself alludes to this text in the institution of the eucharist (*Mark* 14:22-25 and parallels). The text of *Jeremiah* 31:31-34 is reproduced here. The prophet draws on a key theme or word of the Old Testament with which his audience would have been very familiar: covenant. This word or concept was in many ways the primary expression of relationship between the Lord and Israel, particularly for the group we identify now as the Deuteronomic school who had such a strong influence on the final form of the *Book of Jeremiah* as we have it now. For the Deuteronomists the word "covenant" expressed all the essentials of Israel's faith: commitment to the Lord, fidelity through observance of the commandments, assumption of obligation, mutual declaration of commitment by oath taking, creation of enduring relationship (*Deuteronomy* 32:45-47). The covenant format used in Israel was simply borrowed from, and elaborated upon, the format common in the Ancient Near East which formalised treaties as well as many commercial enterprises. The Deuteronomists adopted and promoted a term familiar from military, political and commercial life in the ANE as the key expression of their understanding of the relationship in faith between the Lord and Israel. Jeremiah is celebrated as one of the great poetic exponents of this covenant relationship in his new covenant text (31:31-34).

JEREMIAH 31:31-34

31 The days are surely coming, says the Lord, when I will make a new covenant with the house of Israel and the house of Judah.

32 It will not be like the covenant that I made with their ancestors when I took them by the hand to bring them out of the land of Egypt – a covenant that they broke, though I was their husband, says the Lord.

33 But this is the covenant that I will make with the house of Israel after those days, says the Lord: I will put my law within them, and I will write it on their hearts; and I will be their God, and they shall be my people.

34 No longer shall they teach one another, or say to each other, "Know the Lord," for they shall all know me, from the least of them to the greatest, says the Lord; for I will forgive their iniquity, and remember their sin no more.

Structure of the passage

We could identify the structure of the passage as follows:

v. 31	announcement of the new covenant
v. 32	negative description, or what the covenant is not
v. 33	positive description
v. 34	consequences of the new covenant

Verse 31: announces the new covenant as the divine initiative. It is not accompanied by or represented by any external ceremony or rite (as was the case with covenants in the Old Testament) as this will be about the transformation of the person as an inner reality. This is a "new" covenant, that is, it assumes familiar forms but it is not simply a new form of the old since the old will be shown to be ineffective. This covenant is inclusive as it is given to both the house of Israel and the house of Judah.

Verse 32: offers a negative description of the new covenant is as much as it identifies features of the old form which will be discontinued because the old covenant has not achieved its purpose. In effect, the Lord announces a break with the Sinai covenant. The positive action of God, the Lord's great deeds of the past (*Deuteronomy* 11:1-7) have met with a consistently negative response from their fathers and because of this persistent infidelity the covenant must change. The old covenant was unable to bring about its desired or intended result.

Verse 33: speaks of the new covenant in positive terms. The emphasis here is on the divine initiative, the quality of the relationship and the mode of covenant. We note the strong pattern of first and third person subjects and verbs and the reciprocal nature between them. This is a direct relationship between the people and God, on an individual basis, which the Lord announces. There is no need for this relationship to be mediated as previously by priest and prophet. This is a direct relationship between the Lord and the individual. Prophet as intercessor and priest as cult mediator are now superfluous. We

> *There is no need for this relationship to be mediated as previously by priest and prophet. This is a direct relationship between the Lord and the individual.*

notice the direct connection the Lord makes between "covenant" and "law". This is a covenant law written not on external clay tablets but on the human heart. What is announced here is a radical transformation of the human heart. There are elements of continuity here: the expression "I will be their God, and they shall be my people" is very familiar from Old Testament covenant texts. There are elements of discontinuity here: the old mode is abandoned (verse 32) and a new mode, written on the heart, is announced.

Verse 34: identifies the consequences of the new covenant. The mode but not the content of the great Sinai covenant (*Exodus* 24) is abandoned. It has not brought about the transformation of the heart so necessary for covenant religion and faith and so a new mode is necessary. The commandments have not been abandoned, simply the mode in which they can be truly observed. God will transform the human heart. Knowledge of God will not need to be taught since all will know the Lord, we might say intuitively. What makes this new mode of covenant possible and efficacious, what enables this magnificent vision and announcement to come about, is divine forgiveness of sin. God removes what effectively blocks the relationship (sin) and at the same time creates the human capacity to respond (transformation of heart). The oracle of the new covenant (31:31-34) does not require the people to do anything: this is all the divine initiative.

A bridge to the New Testament

In commenting on this celebrated text of the new covenant in Jeremiah we might simply say that if the bridge between the Old Testament and the New Testament is to be understood largely in terms of prophecy and the fulfilment of prophecy, as many of the writers in the New Testament suggest (see *Luke* 4:14-21), then this text of the new covenant, similar to the text of the fourth Song of the Servant (*Isaiah* 52:13-53:12), is one of the principal bridges used by the Holy Spirit to bring the two testaments together and to present the ministry of Jesus in its full prophetic and salvific significance.

above: Babylon (Victorian woodcut)

SUMMARY

- Jeremiah was (like Moses) a reluctant prophet.

- He ministered in the kingdom of Judah in the late seventh and early sixth centuries BCE.

- Against the background of the rise of Babylon as the new superpower in the region, Jeremiah lived in troubled and uncertain times.

- He was an eyewitness to some of the great watershed events of the sixth century, such as the two sieges of Jerusalem by the Babylonians in 597 BCE and 587 BCE.

- Jeremiah gives the reader access to his inner life, his relationship with God in prayer and the personal hardship involved in being a prophet of the Lord.

- His prophecy consists of oracles, prose speeches and biographical narratives.

- The famous new covenant text (31:31-34) is the second most quoted Old Testament text in the New Testament, after Psalm 110.

- Covenant was one of the key words for Jeremiah with all its connotations of commitment, fidelity, obligation and enduring relationship.

Chapter Five

Ezekiel

Divine Presence in Absence

Prophet
Ezekiel

Description
Priest and prophet out of place and out of time

Occupation
Priest

Time of ministry
Sixth century BCE

Place of ministry
Among the exilic community in Babylon

Message
Despite His seeming absence, God is present with the exilic community.

❦ Therefore prophesy, and say to them, thus says the Lord God: I am going to open your graves, ... and I will bring you back to the land of Israel. ❦

Ezekiel 37:12

Ezekiel: prophet of exile

Ezekiel was a younger contemporary of the prophet Jeremiah, although we can only conjecture as to whether they actually met. Both witnessed the first Babylonian siege of Jerusalem in 597 BCE. Ezekiel was taken as a prisoner into exile in Babylon in the first deportation after the surrender of the city. He lived with his fellow exiles in the Judean community in Babylon and died there. He was the prophet of and to the exilic community. The *Book of Ezekiel* gives us some good information about the life and circumstances of the prophet. He was a priest (1:3) and lived in the exile settlement near the river Chebar in Babylon (1:1-3). The famous refrain from Psalm 137 comes to mind: "By the rivers of Babylon – there we sat down and there we wept when we remembered Zion". His call as a prophet occurred several years into his exile in the year 593 BCE (1:1-3). The last dated oracle we have from the prophet can be dated to 571 BCE (29:17). His call narrative (1:1-3:15) is an extended, complex, highly visual account of his vision of the Lord on a throne chariot, attended by heavenly beings, an account which may have drawn upon sources of Babylonian astrology. The *Book of Ezekiel* says little about the confrontation of the Judean community with its Babylonian environment and culture. This confrontation is to be found in Second Isaiah (*Isaiah 40-55*).

Vision narratives

Visions are key to understanding Ezekiel's prophecy. In the *Book* there are three great vision narratives: 1:1-3:15, the call narrative; 8-11, the sins of Jerusalem and the departure of the divine presence from the doomed temple; and, 40-48 the new sanctuary of the divine presence. In each of the visions Ezekiel is presented as an active

participant. Much of the prophecy is written in the first person. Actions and gestures are important in his prophetic message. We might speak of these actions (and especially in the call narrative vision in 1:1-3:15) as auto-dramatic, that is, the prophet acts out in his own person the fate of his people, as revealed by the Lord. Such personal investment in the message, then, is more than simply pantomime. Priesthood, priestly language and cultic ritual are also important in understanding the *Book*, particularly the associated themes of divine holiness and divine presence/absence. There is great attention to precise details and dates of oracles — some fourteen such dates are given — although not in chronological order. Ezekiel was a sensate. Materials in the *Book* might strike the modern reader now as bizarre and fantastic, even offensive. Ezekiel was clearly an intense and complex person.

An outline of the Book of Ezekiel

Like many of the other prophetic books of the Old Testament, the *Book of Ezekiel* reveals an extended process of editing and redacting by the prophet himself and by disciples of his school to produce the book we have now in final form. We cannot simply discount Ezekiel's direct role as the author of many of the oracles and prose sections of the *Book,* with the exception of chapters 40-48. The *Book* reveals a clear enough structure which we could outline in general terms as follows:

"The upholder of holiness ..."
Pedersen

The principal task of the prophet in Israel was not to foretell the future but to be the messenger of the Lord to the community, bringing words of judgement, of consolation or of hope. The prophet was an intercessor (Deuteronomy 18:9-22). His task was to call Israel back to holiness, understood as fidelity to covenant religion. The quintessential quality of God is holiness. Israel was called to be holy (Leviticus 20:26). The prophet's task was to uphold and to promote holiness. Naturally, this demanded that the prophet be a holy person himself.

Structure of the Book of Ezekiel

1:1-3:15 call narrative and first theophany or vision of the divine presence

3:16-21 Ezekiel is designated "watchman"

3:22-5:17 symbolic, auto-dramatic actions related to the 587 BCE siege of Jerusalem

8:1-11:25 second theophany or vision of the departure of the divine presence from the doomed city and temple

15-17, 23 allegories of the vine, Jerusalem as whore, the eagle, the two sisters

24 announcement of the siege of Jerusalem by Neduchadnezzar

25-3 oracles against the nations

34-37 oracles announcing the coming salvation of the Lord

40-48 third theophany or vision of the new temple and the return of the divine presence to the sanctuary

above: Ezekiel drawing a chart to show the seige of Jerusalem

right: cherubim and chariot vision of Ezekiel

Again, revealing its structure and the specific context of exile and the siege/destruction of Jerusalem as historic events around which much of the material in the *Book* is organised, we note that the *Book of Ezekiel* could be read in general terms in two parts: chapters 1-24 contains materials before the second and final siege of Jerusalem in 588-587 BCE, that is, materials which relate to the years 593-588 BCE, while chapters 25-48 contain materials after the fall of the city, that is, materials which relate to the period 586-571 BCE. The commencement of the second Babylonian siege of Jerusalem is clearly announced in Ezekiel's prophecy in 24:1-2, while the fall of Jerusalem is announced to the prophet by a fugitive from the city in 33:21. The siege and capture of Jerusalem is a pivotal event in the *Book of Ezekiel*; one might describe it as a traumatic event.

The Book of Ezekiel as trauma literature

One of the ways in which some modern commentators of the *Book of Ezekiel* are beginning to read the work is as trauma literature. This is a useful insight into the *Book*. The traumatic nature of what is presented here relates both on a personal level to the prophet Ezekiel himself, as well as on a national level to his exilic community and the community in Judah after 597 BCE. There is much in the *Book* which we might describe as trauma. We begin with the prophet himself. Ezekiel is never addressed by the Lord by his own proper name as other prophets have been (*Jeremiah* 1:11; *Amos* 7:8). Instead, the Lord calls him "mortal", "son of man" or "watchman" (3:16-17). Ezekiel was taken as a captive away from his homeland. Apart from his return in visions (8:1-9:11), we have no reason to believe he ever saw Jerusalem and his homeland again. He suffered the trauma of exile and loss. Further, in the profane land of exile

and with no temple Ezekiel could not exercise his priesthood. He underwent a significant shift in his self-understanding from priest to prophet. His wife died suddenly and he was forbidden to mourn for her. Instead her death was to be interpreted as an allegory of the forthcoming destruction of the Jerusalem temple (24:15-27). His call narrative reveals bizarre ordeals and actions which he must perform as metaphors of the forthcoming siege of Jerusalem (3:22-5:17) including cooking his meals over human dung (4:12). Ezekiel finds this command repulsive. It could be fairly suggested that in the vision sequences in chapters 1-3 and 8-11 Ezekiel is in a virtual catatonic state (8:3). While the categories of modern psychology may not be entirely appropriate to his person and situation, it would nevertheless be fair to suggest that Ezekiel was a highly developed sensate, a person whose behaviour bordered on the obsessive compulsive, and a person damaged by dislocation and loss. Ezekiel lived through trauma.

A community copes with trauma

This same traumatic pattern is also evident in the *Book* on the level of the fate of Judah and Jerusalem, and particularly the second and final siege of the city. Trauma is portrayed not just on a personal level for Ezekiel the prophet but also on a national level for his fellow exiles, fellow countrymen and co-religionists. The horrors of the 588-587 BCE siege of Jerusalem including starvation and cannibalism are graphically portrayed (4:1-5:17). The capture of the city by the Babylonians signals the end of the state of Judah, the punishment and exile of its last king, King Zedekiah, the destruction of the temple of Solomon and the city walls, and further exile of its peoples (*Jeremiah* 39:8-10). These are portrayed as catastrophic events. This is a community reeling from unimagined loss, with little idea of its future, with a profound sense of having been abandoned by the Lord, struggling to comprehend what has happened. This is a community in trauma. Ezekiel shares this profound sense of loss. He graphically portrays the history of his people's relationship with the Lord as one of constant infidelity (23:1-49; 16:1-63). While destruction of city and state may be the (just) punishment for sin and apostasy (8:1-9:11), Ezekiel and his fellow Judeans experience these events as traumatic.

A vision of hope: the bones in the valley (37:1-14)

As we have seen with the general structure of the *Book,* the first part tends to be the standard prophetic "doom and gloom" while the second part is more hopeful. The capture of Jerusalem is the event which signals a change in the structure of the *Book*. After the fugitive arrives with the news, Ezekiel is again able to speak (33:21-22). What follows in chapters 34-48 generally are hopeful oracles of a new future. Significant among these oracles of hope is the famous text of the vision of the valley full of bones (37:1-14). This text is a vision narrative, similar to the other such narratives in the *Book*. It consists of two parts: the image of the valley full of bones (verses 1-10) and the interpretation of the vision (verses 11-14). The Lord brings the prophet Ezekiel in a vision to a valley full of the bones of dead men. There are vast quantities of the bones and they are very dry. The Lord orders the prophet to prophesy over the bones to bring them to life. A vast army is resurrected. The Lord then interprets the action for the prophet: the army of bones represents the house of Israel which believes it is as good as dead. The Lord announces a new future: revivification and resettlement in their own land. The vision concludes decisively (verse 14). We note that Ezekiel participates actively in the vision: seeing, responding, acting. Let us look at the text of the vision more closely, verse by verse.

Verse 1: The prophet is brought by the spirit of the Lord into a dramatic setting of a valley full of bones. The words "spirit" and "breath" occur frequently in the text. Ezekiel has been seized by the Lord in this vision, that is, inspired.

Verse 2: Ezekiel is, as it were, clambering over all the bones. There are many bones and they are very dry, suggesting a vast multitude of slain who have been dead for a long time. Suggestions of revivification seem pointless.

Verse 3: In the question and answer pattern between the Lord and the prophet human incapacity and divine power are placed side by side.

Verses 4-5: Ezekiel is commanded by God to prophesy over the bones. God's creating breath/spirit will enter the dry bones.

Verse 6: This revivification will take place in two stages, firstly with enfleshment and secondly with the living spirit. We are reminded of the narrative of the creation of the human beings in the *Book of Genesis* (2:7). In this re-creation human beings will "know the Lord".

Verse 7: The prophetic word brings about what it announces. The bones rattle together and the human skeletons take recognisable shape and form.

Verse 8: Similar to the *Genesis* account, the reconstituted bodies have physical shape but they lack the breath of life which only the Lord can give.

Verse 9: God commands Ezekiel to prophesy and fill the bodies with the breath of life in order to become living beings.

Verse 10: Again, the prophetic word, once announced, achieves its designated purpose and the army becomes living beings, a vast multitude of living beings. We are reminded of another Old Testament text (*Daniel* 12:1-4) which speaks of resurrection of the dead in terms of standing upright.

Verse 11: The Lord offers an interpretation of this action. God quotes the words of the people themselves: we are as good as dead! We have no hope!

Verses 12-13: God has not forgotten this people. They are literally raised from their grave of hopelessness and restored to their land.

Verse 14: The divine motive for doing this action is clear: "that you may know that I am the Lord". God's spirit will be in them and they will live again in their own land.

SUMMARY

- Ezekiel was a contemporary of Jeremiah, and like that prophet was a priest.

- Exiled to Babylon in 597 BCE, he became the prophet to the exilic Jewish community after receiving a prophetic call/vision several years into his exile.

- There are three great vision narratives in the Book of Ezekiel in chapters 1-3 (call narrative), 8-11 (vision of the doomed Jerusalem), and 40-48 (new temple).

- A good way of understanding the Book of Ezekiel for us today is to see it as trauma literature, both for the prophet himself and his exilic community.

- Ezekiel's prophetic message does not consist only in words but in actions and gestures in which he actively participates.

- The vision of the dry bones (37:1-14) brought back to life as a symbol of the revivified community in Judah is one of the great Old Testament texts.

Chapter Six

Isaiah

AND HIS CHILDREN

Prophet
  Isaiah
Description
  Proclaimer of divine holiness
Occupation
  Priest
Time of ministry
  Eighth century BCE
Place of ministry
  Jerusalem
Message
  God is holy and looks for holiness among his people in their commitment to social justice.

See, I and the children whom the lord has given me are signs and portents in Israel from the Lord of hosts, who dwells on Mount Zion.
Isaiah 8:18

Isaiah and the Messiah

The *Book of Isaiah* is generally regarded as a composite work of (at least) three authors or "Isaiahs" over several hundred years. Our concern here now is with the first Isaiah (chapters 1-39 of the *Book*), a prophet who ministered in Jerusalem in the eighth century before Christ. Some of the better known texts of first Isaiah are the so-called Messianic prophecies to be found in chapters 7-11 of the *Book*. These texts occur in the Advent readings of the liturgy each year. As well, the texts are the basis of Handel's great oratorio *Messiah*, sung each Advent by professional choirs throughout the world. Messianism became an increasingly important ideological belief in the Old Testament and so we need to clarify its meaning in order to understand something of Isaiah's use of this ideology in the prophecies. The scholar Joseph Fitzmyer offers a helpful definition of the term "Messiah" when he writes; "The term expresses a notion that emerged in Palestinian Judaism in pre-Christian centuries and denoted an eschatological figure, an *anointed* human agent of God, who was to be sent by Him as a deliverer and was awaited in the end time." (*The One Who Is To Come.* Grand Rapids, MI: Eerdmans Publishing Company, 2007, 1). This definition emphasises four key aspects of this messiah figure: a person associated with the *eschaton* or definitive breaking into history of God's reign, a human being (not divine) who has been anointed or consecrated for a mission, sent by God as a deliverer of his people (not necessarily political figure), and who would come at the end of time. Messianism in Isaiah is associated with royal messianism, that is, its association with the house of David. The New Testament used this ideology, in a guarded fashion, as a theological lens or filter through which to understand the life and ministry of Jesus. The key messianic texts in first Isaiah are 7:1-17; 9:1-7; 11:1-9.

Children in messianic texts

These texts in Isaiah need to be situated in a specific historical context in order to be properly appreciated. The historical context is the Syro-Ephraimite war of 735-732 BCE. Basically, the kings of Damascus and Ephraim (or Samaria) had besieged Jerusalem in order to remove Ahaz, King of Judah (736-716 BCE) and replace him with a more amenable ally. Ahaz appealed to the protection of the Assyrian emperor and became his vassal *(2 Kings* 16:1-20). The three messianic texts describe encounters between the prophet Isaiah and Judean kings. In each text or scene a child is present who bears a provocative or symbolic name(s) and whose presence becomes a sign. None of the children speak. The prophecy invites the reader to focus on the presence of the child, the name of the child and the sign value of the child, that is, the significance, the meaning and the importance of the prophecy that emerge by focussing on the child, rather than the adults. Some of these children are Isaiah's children. We can briefly consider each of the three texts.

> *"We shall understand "prophet" to mean a purely individual bearer of charisma, who by virtue of his mission proclaims a religious doctrine or divine commandment."* Max Weber
>
> *Weber was a sociologist rather than a commentator on scripture. Nevertheless, this statement has a number of important insights into Israel's prophets in the Old Testament. The prophet was first of all a charismatic individual, that is, a person with a gift for public utterance or discourse. Secondly, the prophet was called not to occupy or continue a religious public office but to undertake a mission (Amos 7:14-16). Thirdly, prophecy has to be understood as a specifically religious phenomenon in as much as the prophet proclaims a message to the community on behalf of God from whom he claims a mandate to speak (Isaiah 6:8-9).*

First messianic text (11:1-9)

The first messianic prophecy is 7:1-17. The prophecy consists of basically three parts: an introduction (verses 1-2), first scene of encounter between prophet and king (verses 3-9), and second scene of encounter (verses 10-17). Verses 1-2 describe the historical context of the Syro-Ephraimite war in which Ahaz perceives his kingdom to be

in grave danger. The first meeting in verses 3-9 (scene 1) describes the commission from the Lord to the prophet Isaiah to meet the king and to reassure him against this threat. Isaiah is accompanied by his son whose name is *Shear-jashub*, a name which means "a remnant shall return" in its Hebrew form. The child does not speak but the scene is centred around the child's presence and the highly symbolic value of his name. The meaning of the child's symbolic name is also spelt out later in the prophecy (10:20-23). The name is not only symbolic but provocative. The king must place his trust and faith in God's word and God's protection: "if you do not stand firm in faith, you shall not stand at all" (verse 9). Ahaz must not rely on political power or rescue (he did, and became the vassal of the Assyrian emperor) but on God's promises *(2 Samuel* 7:16).

In the second meeting between Ahaz and Isaiah (verses 10-17), the king is invited to ask a sign from the Lord, a sign of confirmation of protection. When the king (piously) refuses, the Lord announces a sign through the ministry of Isaiah: it is the sign of the Immanuel child. The text invites the reader to focus on the name and role of the child, rather than the child's identity. The child's name is Immanuel, a name which means "God-is-with-us" (8: 8,10). The child (royal?) shall eat curds and honey, in itself an ambivalent sign/menu since it may signify royal food or the food of bare subsistence (*Deuteronomy* 32:13-14). The child will share the fate of his people. The meaning and consequences of the Immanuel sign name are spelt out in verses 18-25. We note the ambivalence associated with the meaning of the child's name and the ambivalence of the sign value of the child. Other children also bear disturbing, provocative names (8:1-4).

Second messianic text (9:1-7)

The second messianic prophecy text is 9:1-7. The text begins by contrasting gloom and darkness (symbols of foreign oppression and occupation) with light in verses 1-2, and all its associations of hope, joy and the future. The yoke of burden will be removed by the Lord. The occasion of this joy is the birth of a royal child. The sign value of the child's birth is indicated in the prophecy in two ways: the titles the child will bear, and the actions the child will perform. Again, the text invites us to focus on the role the child will perform and its sign value, rather than on the child's identity. The child bears a string of lyrical names: Wonderful Counselor, Mighty God, Everlasting Father, Prince of Peace. These titles do not signify that the child is divine but rather are based upon, and draw from, formal liturgies and ceremonies associated with the installation of a king. The birth of a royal child of the Davidic line gives a dispirited people hope (verse 7). The other way in which the sign value of the child's presence is important is in terms of what the child will do: he will perform justice and righteousness. The key duty of Israel's kings (sadly, not performed by most) was to exercise justice and righteousness for the people as the true basis of society (*Jeremiah* 22:15-16). This child will perform justice and righteousness for his people. The prophecy celebrates God's deliverance and the establishment of a Davidic king (*2 Samuel* 7:14).

Third messianic text (11:1-9)

The third messianic prophecy text in Isaiah is 11:1-9. This text is possibly the best known of the three prophecies. The text appears to be in three parts, each part synchronised with the others in order to from a synthetic whole. The text celebrates the ideal Davidic king. The first part (verses 1-3a) celebrates the divine endowment for the king's rule. This ruler will not base his authority on political power or might but on his use of the gifts of the spirit of the Lord, gifts of wisdom, understanding, counsel, might and knowledge. The second part of the prophetic oracle (verses 3b-5) speaks of the character or quality of the king's rule which will be that of justice, righteousness, faithfulness, and especially for the poor as the most vulnerable persons in the kingdom. The third part of the oracle (verses 6-9) speaks of the fruits or consequences of this just rule: security and peace in society. This aspiration is expressed lyrically in the oracle with an Eden-like harmony between all the animals of the earth in which the strong do not prey on the weak and in which seeming opposites find an harmonious unity together. This is a splendid vision of peace. This messianic ruler is from the house of David: "a shoot shall come out from the stump of Jesse" (verse 1). The image of the small shoot indicates this is a child descendant. This ruler will be a servant. As "the spirit of the Lord shall rest on him" (verse 2), this ruler shall be endowed with divine-like qualities: capacity to understand, to perceive, to act justly, to be attentive to human need, to be dependable. His authority does not rest on his political power but on God's endowment of special gifts. What results is a harmony in creation.

Focus is on children

Each of these celebrated messianic prophecies of Isaiah focuses on children. In each oracle we are invited to focus on the presence of the child in the scene(s), on the name(s) the child bears, and on the sign value for the adults the child embodies. In each there is a correlation between the meaning of the child's name and his presence in that scene. As we have seen, each of these oracles is complex and ambivalent, suggesting many levels of related meanings. This is poetry rather than prose narrative. Isaiah is not interested in issues of identification but in eliciting hope and faith in God's promises from a dispirited people who live under the threat of the Assyrian superpower to the north and who need to be reassured that God will be faithful to his promise, particularly to the Davidic dynasty, and that a society of stability, peace and harmony is not beyond their grasp. Why children? Because the child is always the symbol of a new generation, of the future, of hope, of contingency and of possibility. Why a sign? Because a sign given by God is always capable of multiple meanings and continuous interpretation. These beautiful lyrical texts invite the audience to renewed faith and trust in God.

SUMMARY

- The Book of Isaiah is a complex work, consisting of oracles from at least three Isaiahs over several hundred years.
- The messianic texts in chapters 7, 9 and 11 are familiar to us from Advent liturgy and from the great choral work 'Messiah' by Handel.
- The focus of these texts is on the presence of children, their symbolic names, and the sign value they represent in each text or scene for the adults present.
- These texts are written in poetry rather than prose.
- Isaiah's intention in composing the texts was to bolster hope and faith in a community under threat from the Assyrian juggernaut to the north.

Conclusion

“ The prophets of Israel were engaging, dynamic, inspired individuals. ”

Why read the prophets of Israel?

Why read the prophets of ancient Israel? What relevance do they have for us today? What can we learn from them? This overview of the phenomenon of prophecy in Israel reveals at least three good reasons why we should read the prophets as relevant for us today: the prophets are engaging characters, their society shows some disturbing familiarity with our own, and they reveal some key truths about how God relates with us and reveals the divine self to us. Let us consider each of these three matters in turn.

The prophets of Israel were engaging individuals

The prophets of Israel were engaging individuals. Their ministry meant they were public performers in word and in action, keen to engage their audience and to persuade them of the veracity and authenticity of the word they spoke from the Lord. They were inspired, uncompromising, charismatic individuals. Fundamental to their ministry was a deep, personal relationship with the Lord. They knew they had to be convinced and convicted by the prophetic word themselves before they presumed to preach that word to others. They were more interested in the present than in the future and that is why their principal role was as intercessor rather than predictor of the future: change was an urgent consideration now rather than a future concern. Too often we read the prophets of Israel as doom and gloom people. Rather, the prophets of Israel were engaging, dynamic, inspired individuals. They continue to speak to us across the millennia of the Judeo-Christian tradition.

A disturbing familiarity with our own society

There is a second reason why the prophets are relevant for us: Israelite society at the time of the prophets bears a striking, even disturbing, familiarity with our contemporary society. The prophets were deeply interested in the role of religion in society. They readily acknowledged, and condemned, the ways in which the religious cult of their time had bankrupted itself and led people astray through corruption and greed (*Hosea* 4:4-11). At the same time, however, they readily intuited the inherent possibilities covenant religion in Israel had to lead people to genuine holiness. The prophets did not invent a new religion; rather, they drew on the genius of Israel's faith to show how justice and righteousness could be possible at every level of society (*Hosea* 6:6). The prophets were keenly aware of the inherent evils in their society: structural violence, corrupt judicial system and exploitation of the weak and defenceless, in short, a fundamental lack of solidarity. People in pursuit of profit and comfort did not care for each other (*Amos* 6:4-7). Those who did protest these evils were cowed into silence (*Amos* 5:13). We recognise, sadly, many of these features in our own societies. The prophets of Israel still speak powerfully to us about the people we are and our priorities.

The God of the prophets is our God too

The God of the prophets was a God who was holy, righteous and merciful. This knowledge of God came from personal relationship. Each of these key qualities of God was reflected in Israel's covenant religion: the community must be holy because God is holy, righteousness is revealed not (necessarily) in piety but in justice, and each person was required to be merciful as God had been merciful to them. This God of the prophets is still a God who speaks powerfully to us today. This is the third reason why the ancient prophets of Israel are relevant. The prophets have a great deal to teach us about our relationship with God and with each other. We can specify this relevance in a number of ways. For example, justice and religion go hand in hand, and religion is a poor substitute for justice (*Amos* 5:21-27). A religious cult which reflects true justice in society is more acceptable to the Lord than a cult which has neglected justice and presents itself as a substitute. And again, a society which has displaced the sacred from its central position is a society which, effectively, has made itself sovereign. God is banished to the periphery. And finally, a society which has forgotten its metanarrative (its story of its beginnings, its key events, significant persons and sacred moments which have made it this people) is a society without a future: "thus a people without understanding comes to ruin" (*Hosea* 4:14). The God of Amos and Hosea is still a God very relevant to us today.

Justice and religion go hand in hand

Perhaps the message of the ancient prophets to their co-religionists and to us today could be summed up in this way: holy places do not make people holy; it is holy people who make a place holy. The prophets were opposed to a mechanical form of religion in which people believed God could be manipulated by a sacrificial system, a belief that religion could be isolated from issues of justice and fairness in everyday life. For the prophets religion and justice went inseparably together. Those who saw religion as mere form tended to see holiness attached to a physical place such that entering the holy place made them a different (a holy) person. For the prophets, holiness was a quality born from integrity of life, reflecting divine holiness. Such a person, by their presence and actions, sanctified a holy place. So, the message for ancient Israel from the prophets is the same message for us: what God looks for is truth, justice, righteousness, holiness of life. The prophets live!

Modern Prophets

We could well ask ourselves the question: are there prophets today in our own societies, people mighty in word and in deed, like the prophets of the Old Testament? Is prophecy still alive? Does the prophetic message and word continue? Who would we identify as prophets today? We could think, perhaps, of people like **Mahatma Gandhi** (1869-1948) who led the

Indian struggle for independence from the British and who was instrumental in ending centuries of British rule. He did this in a non-violent fashion and through a program of civil disobedience. He was assassinated on his way to afternoon prayers. Or we might think of **Nelson Mandela** (1918-2013) whose story is still fresh in the minds of many people. Mandela was imprisoned in South Africa for many years because of his opposition to the policy of apartheid. He led his country skilfully through the transition from apartheid to majority rule, becoming South Africa's President. His country avoided much of the bloodshed which may have come with this historic transition. Or we might think of **Martin Luther King** (1929-1968) the great advocate of civil rights for African Americans in the United States. A skilled and inspirational speaker, King inspired a generation of young African-Americans to work for recognition of civil rights for all through the change of law. We might also think of **Aung San Suu Kyi** (1945-) who endured years of house arrest in Myanmar to bring about democratic change in her country and whose dignified and persistent opposition to military rule inspired so many of her countrymen.

Of course, we have our own Australian prophets too. We might think of **Caroline Chisholm** (1808-

1877), an Englishwoman who worked in a determined fashion to improve the welfare and conditions of female immigrants coming to Australia in the nineteenth century. We might also think of **Vincent Lingari** AM (1908-1988), Aboriginal rights activist and member of

the Gurindji people. Etched into Australian historical memory now is the iconic image of Prime Minister Gough Whitlam pouring soil into Lingari's outstretched hands as a sign of recognition of ownership of land. Lingari was a quiet, determined man who brought about legal recognition of Aboriginal ownership of land. Or we might think of **Mary MacKillop** (1842-1909) who founded an order of Catholic religious women to work for education of children in the Australian outback. One of her famous sayings is: "never see a need without doing something about it". Mary also has the distinction of being Australia's first canonised saint (2010).

All of these persons and whoever else we might similarly identify as a prophet of our own times seem to have a number of things in common. These persons challenge and inspire others; they shatter complacency and the easy option favoured by most people of just letting things be. They work for change. Each of these persons too believes in the inherent dignity of every person, that is, human and civil rights belong to each one of us because of who we are and not because these rights have been (grudgingly) given to us by government or authority. This conviction is clearly true for persons like Gandhi, Mandela and King but also for Chisholm and MacKillop who may not have been civil rights activists as such but whose work was clearly based on the dignity of each person. We notice too that all the prophets we have identified here were people who worked for change through non-violent means. They rejected violence as the way of bringing about civil change and opted instead for civil disobedience or civil protest as the way of changing the law. Both Gandhi and King were assassinated. Finally, we note that many of these persons saw their life's work or mission within a higher or decidedly religious context and sought inspiration from their faith and belief for what they were doing: Gandhi was a devout Hindu; King was an ordained minister; Mary MacKillop was a religious sister. Despite their differences of time and place, all of these prophets have a number of things in common. They all believed that the future is what we choose to make it,

a prophet mighty in deed and word before God and all the people (Luke 24:19)

for ourselves and for others.

Many centuries may in fact separate Amos and Hosea from Mandela and Lingari but the prophetic impulse persists. The same concerns, the same questions, the same drive for change, for a sense of solidarity with others, for a sense of the divine in the human enterprise continue. Nearly three thousand years ago Amos and Hosea asked their contemporaries: at what social and economic cost to the poorer members of society has this prosperity been achieved? The question has a disturbing and burning relevance for us. Who are your prophets? Who are the people mighty in word and in deed before God and all the people today?

References used in this text

Quotes from McKane, Kuenen, Pedersen and Wellhausen, are from William McKane, *A Late Harvest: Reflections on the Old Testament*, Edinburgh: T & T Clark, 1995.

Quote from Weber is from David Petersen, *Prophecy in Israel: Search for an Identity*, Philadelphia: Fortress Press, 1987.

Quote from Skinner is from John Skinner, *Prophecy and Religion: Studies in the life of Jeremiah*, Cambridge University Press, 1963 (reprint).

Reference to Blenkinsopp is to Joseph Blenkinsopp, *Sage, Priest, Prophet: Religious and Intellectual Leadership in Ancient Israel*, Louisville, KY: Westminster John Knox, 1995.

GLOSSARY

Assyria—one of major Superpowers of the Ancient Near East, a constant military threat to the kingdoms of Israel and Judah. Ancient Assyria is now modern day Syria and northern Iraq.

Asherahs and Baals—fertility gods of the Canaanite peoples who were seen as important in guaranteeing the cycle of nature (particularly rainfall) in largely agricultural societies like Israel. Prophet Hosea targeted the Baals cult and worship particularly.

Babylon—another of the major Superpowers of the Ancient Near East who menaced Israel and Judah. At the battle of Carchemish in 605 BCE the Babylonian Prince Nebuchadnezzar (later king), destroyed the Egyptian army and Babylon became the major power in the Biblical world of the sixth centuries BCE.

Canon of the Bible—the list of books regarded as inspired by God and having a regulatory authority for life and belief. The Christian canon contains books of both the Old and New Testaments. The Hebrew canon contains the equivalent list of books of the Christian Old Testament canon.

Charism—a gift of God to an individual for the purpose of social and religious leadership of the community. Prophets would be regarded as charismatic individuals.

Cult—the official liturgy and worship of God in the Jerusalem temple. The prophets condemned the misuse of the cult. Several of the prophets were priests themselves.

Day of the Lord—a belief that God would intervene dramatically in the course of history to establish the divine reign. Generally held to be a positive divine initiative, prophets like Amos turned the idea into a day of judgement and doom (see *Amos* 5:18-20).

Decalogue—another name for the ten commandments given by God to Moses as regulating moral and religious behaviour.

Deuteronomic Reform—name given to an important religious reform of cult and faith in the seventh and sixth centuries BCE. Two of its greatest supporters were the kings Hezekiah and Josiah. The reforms of Josiah are described in *2 Kings* 22-23 in the Bible.

Egypt—the third of the great Superpowers of the Ancient Near East, together with Assyria and Babylon. The kingdoms of Israel and Judah were effectively buffer states between the three Superpowers, all vying for control of the region. Israel and Judah were often vassal states of these Superpowers.

Eschatology—specialised term referring to the end time (eschaton) and the dramatic intervention of God in human history.

Exile—name given to the traumatic experience of significant numbers of the Jewish community in Judah who were relocated to Babylon after the capture and destruction of Jerusalem in 587 BCE. The exile lasted until the edict of Cyrus in 538 BCE permitting the Jews to return home (now called Yehud).

Hebrew Bible—sacred scriptures of the Jewish people, generally corresponding to the Old Testament of the Christian bible. The prophets occupy a key position in the Hebrew bible.

Israel—term used in two senses here. Firstly, as a generic name for the audience addressed by the prophets in their oracles, and secondly, as the name of the northern kingdom with its capital Samaria.

Judah—name of the southern kingdom with its capital Jerusalem. The empire of David and Solomon split after the death of Solomon (922 BCE) into the two kingdoms of Israel and Judah. The northern kingdom was absorbed into the Assyrian empire as a province in 722 BCE. The southern kingdom survived until its destruction by the Babylonians in 587 BCE.

Metanarrative—term used in modern narrative critical studies meaning the underlying story of a culture/people. Applied to the bible it means the saving story of the people of the Old Testament and particularly key events like the exodus from Egypt and the giving of the law to Moses at Sinai. Such events describe a people's identity as well as their history. Hosea uses metanarrative in his prophecy, the key dynamic being remembrance.

Messiah—used and applied to chapters 7-11 of the book of *Isaiah* particularly, the term refers to a charismatic individual, associated with the royal house of David, sent by God to bring deliverance to his people, and associated with the end time (eschaton).

Monotheism—belief in the one God, as expressed in the famous *Shema* prayer of Judaism (see *Deut* 6:4-9). Polytheism is the belief in many gods. Prophecy preached monotheistic belief. The perceived danger to monotheism for the prophets was syncretism.

Old Testament—name given to that part of the Christian bible which is the equivalent of the Hebrew scriptures. The Hebrew canon contains most of the books of the Christian Old Testament canon. The Hebrew canon does not contain a New Testament.

Prophet—name or title given in the sacred scriptures to those charismatic, inspired individuals who acted as God's messengers to the community. Prophets fulfilled the roles of intercessors with God for the people and as upholders of the call to holiness through covenant fidelity, rather than as predictors of the future.

Prophecy—the charismatic phenomenon which played such a vital role in Israel's faith and belief between the eighth and sixth centuries BCE.

Prophetic school—term used to describe the school or circle of followers who gathered and edited the oracles of a prophet, sometimes beyond his lifetime, to ensure the message of the prophet endured for subsequent generations. We can speak of schools associated with prophets such as Amos and Hosea.

Redactor—a person or school who acted as editor of the written oracles and messages of a prophet with the purpose of arranging the materials thematically and presenting the forceful relevance of the prophet's teachings for subsequent generations.

Syncretism—defined as the absorption of pagan elements and practices into pure monotheistic faith. The prophets identified syncretism as the major threat to Israel's faith not only because of the ways in which it undermined monotheistic belief but also because of its seeming innocuous appeal in the popular imagination. The setting up of Asherahs in the temple and the worship of the Baals are examples of syncretistic behaviour.

Temple—name given to the principal shrine of the worship of God in Jerusalem, also known as Solomon's temple.

Torah—term used to describe the first five books of the bible (*Genesis, Exodus, Leviticus, Numbers, Deuteronomy*) in the Hebrew canon. Also known as the law of Moses. The term corresponds to the Pentateuch in the Christian bible. More than simply law, Torah means blessing associated with obedience to a way of life.

Trauma theory—a modern sociological and psychological term/theory which some modern bible commentators apply to the books of *Ezekiel* and *Jeremiah* as illustrative of the profound personal damage brought about by dislocation, loss and warfare.

www.ingramcontent.com/pod-product-compliance
Lightning Source LLC
Chambersburg PA
CBHW061059170426
43199CB00025B/2938